9/4

ERIK THE RED

ERIK THE RED

*The Atlantic alone
in a home-made boat*

DONALD RIDLER

WILLIAM KIMBER · LONDON

First published in 1972 by
WILLIAM KIMBER & CO. LIMITED
Godolphin House, 22a Queen Anne's Gate
London, SW1H 9AE

TYPESET BY
SPECIALISED OFFSET SERVICES LTD., LIVERPOOL,
AND PRINTED IN GREAT BRITAIN BY
REDWOOD PRESS LIMITED, TROWBRIDGE

Contents

List of Illustrations

Acknowledgements

To those who gave help, encouragement, and hospitality on the way.

To those in authority who did not exceed it.

To those friends who cannot be mentioned in this book but who are preserved in my memory.

A few names:

Ernie Hill, Robin Hall.

Mr and Mrs Ince, Dr and Mrs Ryan, Major and Mrs Sandeman.

John T. Rowland for the plans.

Harold Wheeler, Peter White, and an unknown, seasick, Portuguese Television cameraman for the photographs.

St James's Secretarial College, Bridport, for the typing.

1. The Idea

To go across an ocean in a boat, to drop the anchor where the shallow sea is sand-white and breaks on palm-blackened beaches, this is a wonderful thing. To go across an ocean in a sailing yacht without an engine, relying only on the force of the wind, the skill of one's arm and the cunning of one's brain, is surely still more wonderful. And for a man to do it in a yacht that he has built himself, must count among the greatest of his dreams and give him a feeling of fulfilment that can be won in no other way.

Perhaps. Perhaps it is only that a deed which is hard to understand seems greater than it is.

I have done this thing. Whether it is worth it, whether the dream turns to a shadow in the end, only time can tell. But if anyone has had this dream and wants it fulfilled, this is how one man fulfilled it.

Where does the dream come from? I suppose I have always been interested in sailing.

I was born during the War in 1941 in Old Trafford, England and grew up the second son of a clergyman. I had two brothers and one sister. This was a large family for my parents to support in the times of rationing and shortage when the fighting had stopped. Because of my father's vocation, it was inevitable that as children we should feel somewhat cut off from other people. Such a feeling has its results in later life. The children of clergymen and policemen often do strange things.

Does it sound bitter to say that I felt cut off and different

from my fellows? It need not. When I look around me, I
often think that this difference is not a bad thing after all.

One of the different things we did took place when my
father had a parish in Suffolk. At one time there were five
churches to run with no curate. Although we lived in the
country where such things are not so needed as in the towns,
it was impossible for him to get a proper holiday away from
his parish. So every summer we used to descend like a pack
of wolves upon a little village called Waldringfield on the
River Deben. The Rector there was a friend of my father, and
he allowed us to camp on a part of his land. He too had four
children around the same age as ourselves, so these gave us
someone else to fight with besides each other.

Every Sunday, and at other times during the week as well,
my father would drive back to Ipswich to tend his parish. But
we children had a marvellous time.

The family boat was a twelve foot open sailing dinghy of a
kind seldom seen today. It was not a racing dinghy. It would
not go fast, except in a strong wind. But it would not turn
over in a gust of wind, it would drive ashore on shingle
without splintering into fragments, it would take a family of
six on expeditions from one side of the river to the other, or
for voyages of several miles up or down it. When one is a
child, the world is a large place, and a trip across a river takes
on all the excitement and adventure of a voyage across
enchanted seas.

The variety of scenery on the Deben makes it one of the
most beautiful rivers in England. Pine-topped sandy cliffs
overshadow sandy beaches, while in other places little creeks
wind their secret ways through saltings of firm river mud and
green samphire. Man has added his touch along the flatter parts
of the scenery. Dykes, or sea walls, stretch along the river,
sometimes broken through in places. Here the high spring tides
would form inland seas, forgotten and ghostly with the dead
bodies of salt-blasted trees standing in the water.

In a few hours, the tide goes out to leave great stretches of
mud. To sail up the channel of the river at this time was like
travelling along a desert track surrounded by quicksands.

Sitting behind a sea wall with the whistle and whisper of the wind through the coarse marram grass. Rollicking filthily through knee-deep black river ooze, bathing it off in the cold English water. Baking in the hot sun behind some cliff sheltering from the chilly East wind and making a silence press upon the buzzing insects. . . .

It is all ordinary enough. We all have such glimpses of the natural world, all of which is beautiful. But these things are what makes us seek to escape from our modern city life, and they grow enough thorns to cushion the bed of a gypsy mind.

The first voyage I made in a yacht happened by chance, due to my younger brother Neil. He had arranged to go from Littlehampton to Gibraltar as crew on an eight ton sailing yacht. But he found at the last moment that he could not go. Could I go instead?

I did.

It was my first voyage at sea. It was often rugged and unpleasant. But nothing can replace the romance of a first voyage at sea.

Black, star-shining nights, with the phosphorescence shooting astern in the warm water like a jet-stream. Bright, spray-filled days, with the sun glinting and sparkling from curving waves and foamy crests. Strong, cold winds, when the boat tosses helplessly in great seas. Hot, breathless calms, when the boat rolls helplessly in an oily swell. . . .

For some people such a voyage would fulfil and cure their wanderlust. For others it only stirs it up, and I was one of these. For me, it strengthened the interest I had always had in boats and the sea.

How was it that I could be so interested in boats and the sea? What urge was it? When I look back, I realize that these things have always been on my mind like a worm in an apple. When I was young I would dream about voyages I would make alone in my own boat, and study the yachting magazines.

About the sea you can say many things. You can talk

about its beauty, the feelings you would have in sailing it, the sense of wild, and forgotten waters, and its ever-changing under your feet. Some people are attracted by it, some are scared by it, while others are attracted by being scared of it.

Certainly a sailing voyage at sea can be insecure and dangerous. This is the price which must be paid for its romance. It is a sad fact that often the things worth doing are those at which most people shrink. And to sail, using the forces of nature and sometimes fighting them, is always satisfying with a satisfaction we have nearly forgotten in this age of machines.

'What a feeling of self-reliance it must bring!' I used to say to myself. 'What a challenge and what a reward — a feeling that you have tested yourself to the full! Surely only then will I be able to treat people with respect, when I no longer feel that I have to depend upon them. For dependence breeds fear, and fear breeds hate.'

All these feelings were aroused even more by the idea of building a boat. What a Robinson Crusoe, Superman feeling would be mine! Wouldn't life be totally different if I could build a boat with my own hands and sail to some, any, foreign shore? Could a man ever be the same again?

I did not know then that the plan might grow even more. And I little realized that the feelings we imagine we will have after an event may turn out in truth to be quite different from those we have expected.

I had left University with a strange feeling of inferiority. At about this time, there was beginning a revolution in thinking. At one time, it was a good thing to have been the son of an earl and unthinkable to be the son of a dustman. Now it was the other way round. Sons of earls used to stagger round with dustbins on their shoulders swearing like troopers in a vain effort to hide their origins. My own particular habit was to try as many jobs as possible, which was almost unthinkable then for an Oxford graduate. This was to satisfy myself that I knew how life really went on. These jobs were always boring, and badly paid. When they became too much to bear, I would get the sack, either through idleness or provocation. I met a lot of people this way, and had a great deal of fun. It was worth doing.

When my parents moved to Dorset, I went to help them to do up a cottage which was attached to the Rectory. After this I obtained a job with a local farmer who eventually and inevitably gave me the sack.

By this time I had about £250 in the bank and was at a loose end, with no idea of what sort of job I really wanted to do.

The village of Burton Bradstock was near the sea and not far from the harbour of West Bay. The garden of my father's rectory was a big one. It seemed a very convenient place to build a boat.

2. The Challenge

I had for many years put by odd pages of a yachting magazine I used to take, called *Yachts and Yachting*. This, in its older days, had a 'do-it-yourself' air. No plush gin-places, no canvas-hung motor boats, chromium-plated ghosts of a sea-faring country, haunted its pages. Instead, it was full of the old-school characters I knew so well. It was navigated by the heaps and the wrecks that we had sailed in. It held good natured scorn for those who could not turn to and splice a rope or caulk a seam, and to build a boat was not such a great thing in its pages. This magazine has changed somewhat now to keep up with the times and the Solent crowd.

The boat I had decided was not beyond my powers to build, was featured in two articles in this magazine. It was a strange looking craft. Designed by an American, John T. Rowland of Maine, it was a twenty-six foot long dory hull with keel and sails.

The dory is part of a sea history which is fast vanishing. It was usually a flat-bottomed rowing boat designed so that several could be stacked inside one another on the decks of Newfoundland Grand Banks cod-fishing schooners. These cockleshells would be dropped over the side with one or two men, armed with long lines, oars, and conch-shell horn to attract attention in fog. When they had done their fishing in these dangerous waters, they would be picked up again by the schooner.

The dory found its shape for various reasons. It is flat-bottomed, with sides flowing outwards to the gunwale, and double ended with raked ends. This shape makes the boats easy to build, yet easy to drive through the water. With the thwarts removed, it enables them to be stacked one inside the other like stacking chairs. In addition, the flare to the topsides makes the boat very stable since it increases its buoyancy as more goes into the water. The greatly pronounced curve upwards to bow and stern, or sheer, and the two pointed ends, these stopped the boat shipping seas over bow or stern.

The boat in my plans was what is known in the United States as a Cape Anne dory, having a flat transom stern. It looked seaworthy and was said to be fairly fast when the wind was on the stern. Above all, being shaped rather like a box, it looked easy to build. I had very little wood-making skill. I had never built a table, far less a boat. The two magazine articles however, told me quite a lot, and I read books and articles on boat building. It did not look too hard.

The boat was designed to be rigged as a ketch, that is with two masts, the after mast or mizen being the smallest. The rigging, since the design was fairly old, looked simple and cheap, but sails, I knew, could be expensive, unless one were lucky enough to find second-hand ones of the right size. Sometimes these turn out to be rotten, if of canvas.

It may sound as if I knew all about yachts and yacht design. This was not so. I know more than I did then, and I write this with the wisdom that comes after the event. Then, I knew only what I had read in books and what I had picked up from a limited experience of sailing. But of course if I had known all the problems to start with, I might never have decided to do such a foolish thing as to build a boat.

My father was not too happy about the idea. He said it was a big job, and in this he knew better than I did. He wrote to a sailing acquaintance of his in Suffolk to ask his advice, saying that he thought I had two hundred and fifty pounds. This man wrote back:—

I am in the timber trade and have been sailing in small boats for many years. I can say definitely that timber prices being what they are today, it is impossible to build a 26 foot boat for £250. I do not expect your son will enjoy being told this. The younger generation today think they know everything, and do not like taking advice from anyone.

There could not be a better way of getting someone to build a boat for £250. I did not like taking advice from him, and I did not take it.

He had a lot on his side. I made a list of the timber I needed. From my books I had learnt where to use oak, or ash or pine. . . .

In the first place, timber yards were very reluctant to produce this timber. They were often quite willing to provide, say an oak tree, but as for cutting it up. . . . It took quite a while for me to accept this point of view.

Secondly, any wood other than pine or deal was looked upon as a freak. If it could be had at all, it was very costly.

Thirdly, even the ordinary deal or pine was absurdly expensive and looked knotty and unseasoned. It went against the grain, so to speak, to pay a high price for this rubbish. I had to think again.

Then I remembered that sometimes one could buy up job lots of old timber. If I was going to use the worst wood, I might as well get it really cheaply. Not knowing anything about boat building the idea did not seem impossible.

I was more or less committed now. If you tend to waver in the face of a difficult enterprise which you have decided upon, it pays to act as if it is already done. If you want to buy a house, make the curtains first. They will act as a reproach to your lack of action. I bought an anchor and chain, a small inflatable dinghy and other bits and pieces. They reproached me for a long time.

To buy old timber was not so easy. Luck counts for a good deal since some people are not good at answering letters. One demolition firm I dealt with in Southampton had a fire which burnt up all their stocks. I had wasted a lot of time waiting for them to deliver. Then another demolition company I tried, offered me timber at a cheaper price than the last.

They had plenty of old timber, so I went down and picked out what I wanted. They delivered promptly. But the next time I tried them, they had nothing at all, due to a business slump.

As timber baulks to act as a base for building the boats, I used old railway sleepers. Twelve of them cost six pounds. There were also odd pieces left by the builders when they were doing repairs on the Rectory. In addition, whenever I walked along the beach I kept my eyes open for driftwood. Nowadays the Chesil Beach is not a very good source, but the two main beams which help to hold the masts up came from there.

Nearly all my timber of course, had nailholes, or nails still stuck into it. All these nails had to be knocked out and any I missed did not improve the tools. The holes left I hoped to be able to block up somehow.

I could not get any pieces for the frames and floors. These were to be 2″ x 2″ for the side frames and 2″ x 3″ or 2″ x 6″ for the floors. The floors are the part of the frames which go across the flat bottom of the hull to hold the planking on.

The planking I had plenty of. This consisted of old floorboards of varying lengths. The width was about 8½″ and the thickness $\frac{7}{8}$″. These would originally have been 1″ thick before planing for their original use, but the passage of feet and the replaning I had to do to them reduced the thickness to ¾″ instead of the specified 1″. I hoped that this would not matter.

So to make the frames and floors, I sawed up many of the planks into thirds or halves, using a saw attachment on a Black and Decker power drill. It took a long time. When there were enough strips, these were glued together to the required thickness and lengths.

Glue is a very important part of boat building for the amateur. It means that a bad carpenter like myself can make perfect joints. Enough glue will fill in all the cracks and spaces a better craftsman would condemn. Also it is claimed to be stronger than the wood itself. The glue I used was

Aerodux 500 made by CIBA Ltd. It comes in three different types, depending upon the temperature it is expected to set at. You must get this right if possible. If you have a fast-setting glue and use it when the weather is warm, the glue will begin to set before you have time to put the two pieces together. A slow-setting glue may take ages to harden in colder weather.

Glue by itself is not enough. Apart from a possible failure of the glue-setting or of the timber itself, it is essential to nail the pieces together to hold the joint in position while the glue sets. Traditionally, boats were fastened with copper nails, these being put right through the joints. A disc was put over the projecting end, this being cut off so as to be almost flush. The end was then hammered so that it would not slip through the disc.

This method is very good, but is expensive and best done with two people. It is also slow. Iron nails are seldom satisfactory, while screws are expensive and slow to put in. I compromised upon Tower Gripfast nails. These were shaped so that they would go in easily, but were almost impossible to withdraw. They could be hammered in like an ordinary nail, held almost as well as screws, and were made of bronze, one of the few metals which stand up to a long life at sea. These fastenings were used to join the separate pieces of frames. To join two strips to make a thicker piece I simply put glue on the two meeting faces and put weights on top, or clamped them together until the glue set. As I could not afford many clamps, this was done by putting a circle of string round the pieces to be joined, putting a stick through the top, and then twisting. It worked.

All this preparation took a long time. Sometimes I thought it would have been quicker to have bought a tree and sawn it up into pieces. Many times I wondered what I was doing it for. After all, as so many people were so anxious to point out, if you want a boat, the best way is to get a job and save some money for a year or two like anyone else. Another way is to write begging letters to as many firms or individuals you think might be able to spare some money and get them to sponsor you, in return for the advertising value, if any.

Neither of those methods appealed to me. Besides at this time, I had no idea of trying to sail across an ocean. The plan was simply to build a boat as cheaply as possible. I had never made anything before, and I suppose the Robinson Crusoe aspect called to me.

It was only slowly that the notion came into my head to sail across the Atlantic. When people heard that I was going to build a boat, they would joke and say:

'You're not going to sail across the Atlantic in it, are you?'

'Why not?' I would say in defence of my creation, and this answer would go on ringing in my head. The question 'why not?' is a very difficult question to answer, and a very foolish question to ask.

So I decided to sail across the Atlantic. Of course, I kept it to myself for as long as I could. Most people don't have as much faith in you as you have in yourself, and their criticisms do nothing to boost your morale when you are at a difficult stage of building. At this stage I had begun to see that I had set myself a very big task. It appeared so formidable that the Atlantic seemed far away indeed. . . .

I had at this time the idea of writing something and my parents kindly let me stay with them so that I could devote time to this. Often I did jobs to try and keep the money coming in. But my parents had to lend me some as well.

It was not always the ideal situation. Even nowadays a country parson has a reputation to keep up, and a village is a place where reputations, like secrets, are hard to keep. I do not much like my private life discussed by all and sundry and I also tried to make it a rule never to be seen with a girl from the village to save gossip.

But it is a mistake to be too secret. We must at least find the right mask to hide behind. Otherwise people will invent a mask to fit the shadows of their own strange thoughts. Though this can be amusing. . . .

Imagine a village such as Burton Bradstock is, a huddle of thatched cottages smartened up now by richer folk come in from elsewhere, and slowly being swallowed up in a sea of bungalows. But such a place, sleepy in the West Country sea air and small with people who seldom travel far away, is a place where you can talk to those you meet in the lanes.

'Hullo there! It's a lovely day, isn't it? Isn't it a lovely day?'

'Yes, it's very nice, really warm today.'

'I think it's going to stay fine today.'

'Yes, I think so. But it is a bit cloudy, isn't it?'

'Yes, it is cloudy. But it'll stay fine, if it doesn't rain. By the way, I heard a lot of banging from the Rectory the other day. What *do* you think is going on?'

'That must be Donald, the Rector's son.'

'Oh yes, Donald. That's the one who's a hermit, they say, we never see him around anywhere. He's . . . odd, they say.'

'Yes, I've heard that he's odd.'

'Well, he *is* odd. He never seems to be doing any work. He isn't ill, is he? He's healthy, isn't he? There's no reason why he shouldn't be doing a job. Why do his parents have him there if he isn't doing a job? That's what *I'd* like to know.'

'I heard he was driving a van the other day.'

'A *van*? Really, driving a van? Well, that *is* odd. Hasn't he been to college or something? Anyway, you wouldn't expect him to be driving a van. But then he's strange. Why is it we never see him with a girl-friend? *I've* never seen him with a girl, have you? If he was ill, well, that's different, but for a healthy man. . . .'

'You know, I think it's beginning to cloud over. It could be going to rain, but I hope not, because it's so much better when it's fine. Though the gardens could do with it. . . . There's that banging again. I wonder what he's doing there. Something's going on. He's got that strange thing in the garden. . . . '

'Yes, *have* you seen that? It really is extraordinary. All covered up with black plastic sheets, it was, at the Church Fete in the garden there so nobody could know what it was. They say he goes in underneath it sometimes. I wonder what he does under there . . . '

'Some people say he's building a boat . . . '

'A boat? Never! He's not a boatbuilder, is he? You don't build boats unless you're a boatbuilder, do you? No, I'd give anything to know what he's up to. He's so *strange!* Haven't you found him strange. . . ?'

But a village is also a place where you can rely on help, on interest, on suggestions. And of all of these I had a great deal.

3. The Building

The moulds were set up about a year after I had first hit on the plan of building the boat.

The plans of the boat included 'offsets'. Those are the dimensions of the boat if it could be sliced neatly into sections exactly 4 ft. thick for the length of the boat. As I was so short of timber, moulds were made out of any old stuff I could get hold of. They looked awful.

The sections of the boat were marked out on the floor of the garage with drawing pins, and thread, and these old pieces of wood nailed together to fit the shapes. There were five moulds including the one for the transom or flat stern, and the pine log for the stem (bought second-hand and the nails removed) was also put into place.

The railway sleepers were put on the ground every four feet, all measurements being as exact as I could manage, and the moulds set up precariously upon them. The hull was to be built upside down, and the moulds had legs which were supposed to bring them exactly the right height to get the proper shape of the boat. It took many hours juggling with a long piece of string, a spirit level, and numerous chocks of wood to get everything right. I hoped the sleepers wouldn't settle too much and disturb the measurements.

The next thing was to put on the stringers. These are the long pieces which fit along the corners of the moulds, the chines and the beam shelves. As I did not have long enough lengths for these, they had to be made up out of several smaller pieces nailed onto the moulds and lashed together while the glue in between could set.

Between these stringers, the frames could be fixed. These were simply flat pieces 2" x 1½" made up from the floor-board strips. Those on the bottom of the boat were deeper. The side pieces (frames) had to be fastened to the bottom pieces (floors) with flat pieces of floorboard, which went by the stylish name of gussets. These, I suppose, should have been bolted together, but I did not have any bolts. They were simply nailed until the glue set hard.

All this took a great deal of work. I was not experienced in the use of tools, and some of mine were rather primitive. If you want to build a boat, you do not need much.

A hammer, a small saw, a large rip saw, screwdriver, chisel, mallet; a plane, a rasp, punches, brace and bit, long auger bits for drilling long holes. An axe or an adze is needed for chopping away large amounts of unwanted timber. A power drill with the various attachments, including a circular saw, I found essential. I had three G-clamps for holding bits of wood together. They were almost enough. Otherwise there is very little needed apart from what is in the standard carpenter's tool kit. Some special tools can be borrowed.

Timber and materials were collected or bought well before I needed them. Before the boat was started, I used to stroll along the beach near our home. Sometimes, though not often, there would be good, useable pieces of timber washed up by the sea. These I would carry home.

Every piece of timber was carefully examined, measured, and earmarked for a particular purpose. Under these circumstances, one tends to become an unforgivable hoarder with an eagle 'eye for any junk, rubbish or lumber which might conceivably be of some use to someone somewhere. If the boat could have been built out of twigs, the birds in the village would have had no nests.

Now and then, to keep some money coming in, I would do a job of some sort. There is not a great deal of scope in the country for this sort of thing, but it is possible. I drove a van delivering hardware round the country. The van was not the same afterwards since I had only just passed my driving test.

I drove an old army lorry over fields for an agricultural

contractor. My job was to drive behind a silage cutter, hitting it as seldom as possible, while the grass was blown in a continuous stream over the windscreen or into the back of the lorry.

Another job I did was to clean toilets at the local caravan site. As my colleague was going to college by day, we started at four in the morning, to give him time to get to his college. Since we were in a half-asleep and dazed condition, the job was quite bearable.

The boat took shape slowly. In the winter time, it was difficult to get one's hands working properly in freezing temperatures. More important was the fact that the glue had to set above a certain temperature. I solved this problem by covering the boat with polythene rick sheets and putting a paraffin heater underneath. In a gale these sheets could not be put on, and the boat was exposed to the elements.

I reckoned that in any seven days available for working at least two would be too wet, or cold, or windy to work in. This made progress very slow. In addition, my lack of woodworking skill meant that every operation was very slow. Sometimes I thought I would never finish.

Almost all the timber I acquired had nails in, and these had to be removed before the tools could be used. Even so, sharpening the plane after hitting an unseen nail in a piece of wood became a matter of course. All the best floorboards which were reserved for the hull planking had to be planed down by hand and this took a lot of time and work.

At about this time, I was lucky enough to meet Ernie. Ernie was a retired shipwright and came to the village to live, after his working life. He was a small man whose cheerful features had become well-known round the village. 'If you can't do someone a bad turn, do him a good one,' he said.

He promised to come round and give his opinion on the boat. I must confess I felt a bit anxious about this, and when he came first, I tried to excuse the roughness of the workmanship.

'You've been looking at it a long time,' was all he said, as he went round carefully inspecting the boat. Although he

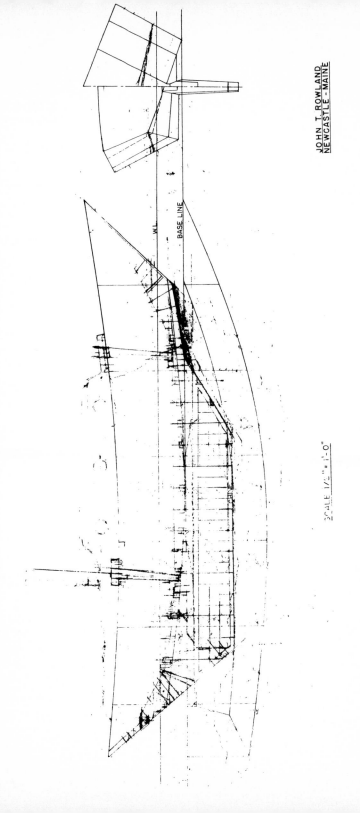

JOHN T. ROWLAND
NEWCASTLE - MAINE

SCALE 1/2" = 1'-0"

Working drawing of the hull of *Erik the Red*

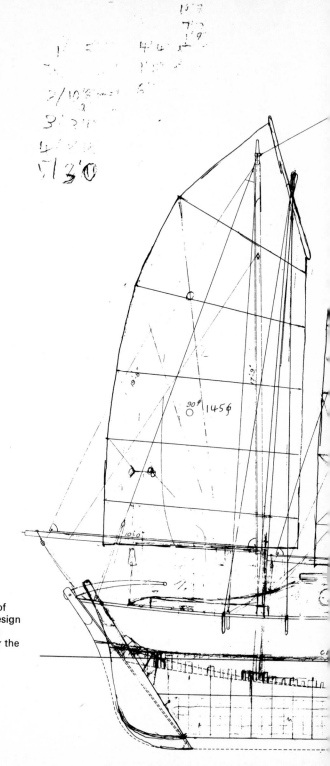

Working drawing of
the rig showing design
for the Chinese rig
superimposed over the
original plan

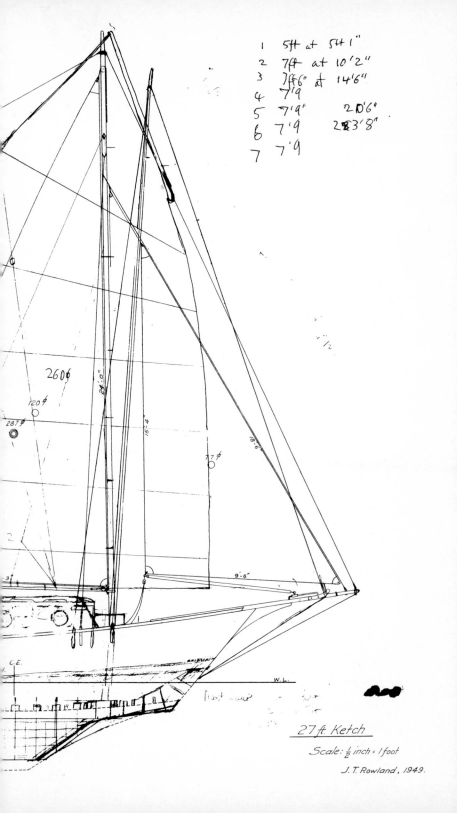

1 5ft at 5ft 1"
2 7ft at 10'2"
3 7ft 6" at 14'6"
4 7'9
5 7'9   20'6"
6 7'9   23'8"
7 7'9

27 ft. Ketch

Scale: ½ inch = 1 foot

J. T. Rowland, 1949.

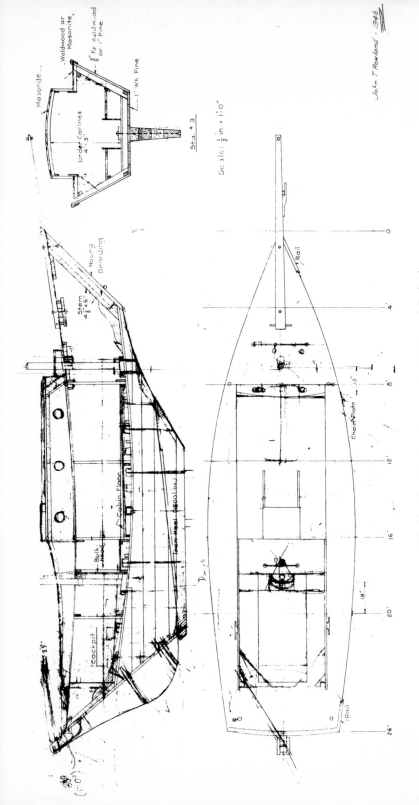

Working drawing showing accommodation and deck-plan

could never have seen a boat made in such a haphazard fashion before, all his criticisms were constructive.

I had now come to the stage of fairing off the frames. To do this, the builder must go round with a long strip of wood. It is clamped onto a frame and then bent round the others. The idea is to plane the frames down until the curved strip fits exactly flush onto their surfaces. When planning the position of the frames, allowance must be made for this, or the boat will turn out a strange shape. Fortunately, I had made no glaring mistakes.

'Go for a fair line,' said Ernie. 'Don't worry about your measurements now.'

It took a long time to get the frames and floors planed down. The thick stempost at the bow also had to have faces planned onto it so that it would exactly fit the planking.

Planking up is quite an exciting part of building a boat. In a boat like this, it is a quick process. The hull is of such a shape that the floorboards fit on without any shaping or bending. All that was needed was to sort out the planks and decide where each one was to go. The flat bottom of the boat was only 20 ft. long down the centre, becoming less towards the chines. Using my longest planks, it was thus simple to have no joins in the planking.

The side planking had to be butted, or joined. Those butts must be planned so that they are spread out throughout the boat, yet are the same on each side. A skill at jig-saw puzzles is a help in this.

The frames being one foot apart, the butt must be put exactly between two of them, joined by a one foot length of planking inside to hold the ends together. These too, are planned before starting, to make sure that one does not turn out to be too long. Since my frames were not as even as they might have been in places, this would not have been surprising.

All the planking was to be glued, being held in place by the barbed ring nails while the glue was setting. For those not familiar with modern glues, I must tell you to start with that these are not like the old-fashioned ones of the past which dissolved in the damp and were a delightful food for wood-eating insects. Modern resorcinol glues are stronger than the wood itself and will last as long. They are not a cheap way of building boats; I spent as much on glue and fastenings as I did on timber. Glue is the one way a non-carpenter like myself can make a perfect joint.

Glueing is a tedious process. First a dry day must be chosen. Then the planks to be fitted are clamped roughly in place and lines drawn round every joint to be glued. This must be done on the frames as well as the planks.

Next, the glue is mixed. The glue I was using was in two parts, which had to be mixed together in equal quantities. I found that the easiest way of doing this was to use an ordinary kitchen measuring jug with the fluid measures marked on it. Half the required quantity was poured in from one can, and half from the other.

This mixture had to be used within about two hours. It meant that fixing joints was always a rush, and any glue, whether on unfixed joints or in the jug, had to be protected from the sun. The glue was smeared onto the pencil lines of one of my planks, the plank was changed into place, and holes for the nails swiftly drilled with the power drill.

This tool made all the difference to working. I would mark the positions of all fastenings with a cross, use the largest drill to put in a counter-sink at every mark, and then drill smaller and deeper holes. The counter-sinking meant that I could hammer the nails beneath the surface of the planking. Later the holes would be stopped with putty.

Often, half-way through this process, the clouds would gather and drops of rain start to fall. Muttering under my breath, I would abandon operations, frantically haul the rick sheets over the boat, each time ripping them a little bit more, and wait for the shower to go by. All this time, the glue in my jug was ageing, so I would fume with impatience.

Then, the shower over, the sheets would be torn off, and work would go on again.

The planks were all fitted edge to edge. During the preparation of each plank, a small chamfer had been planed along the outside of the edges. Thus, when two planks were fitted together, there was a small vee, an eighth of an inch wide to leave room for caulking. Because of my rather haphazard planing, the gaps varied a little, and as the planking dried out in the summer, some gaps became larger. On the whole, though, I was surprised at how well things were going.

The first planks to be fitted were on the bottom of the boat, or the top part when building. The edges of these at the chines were faired off, so that the lower side planks would fit over them.

Once the planking was on, the boat seemed almost done. I did not know then that I had hardly started.

4. Launching

Apart from the primitive materials that the boat was built with, there were two ways in which I had changed its construction drastically. Both were fairly uncommon in the world of yachts, so both tended to worry me somewhat.

The first was the keel. In the original design a long wooden false keel built up of logs was attached to the bottom of the boat. On the bottom of this was a cast iron ballast keel of 1500 lb. The dimensions of this iron keel were given, so that the builder could make his own form for the foundry mould, thus lowering the cost. I wrote to get a foundry quotation. It came to nearly £100. This would put the cost of the keel out of all proportion to the rest of the boat. I decided that I could do one of two things.

A lead keel was a possibility. Lead is the best material for a keel and, unlike iron, is possible to cast oneself. A wooden mould can be made, and out of this a concrete mould made into which to pour the lead. For the bolt holes, plaster of Paris casts are made and fixed exactly in position. After casting, they can be broken out.

The actual heating and pouring of the lead seemed a formidable task but it was quite possible. The cost was against it. Of course, if one is building a boat as an investment, lead might be useful. If the boat became a complete wreck, one could in theory remove the keel and trade it in. Unfortunately, not every ship-wreck is attended by a crane for the purpose of removing lead keels. And if the boat sinks, one is hardly in the position of being able to hump three quarters of a ton of lead keel into the dinghy and row gloatingly ashore with it. So lead, though cheaper than iron was not ideal.

The cheapest keel seemed to be one made of concrete. I had heard of such things. When I was a child sailing in Suffolk, I had had pointed out to me a boat being sold by a local boat-yard worker. This ingenious gentleman had found an old abandoned boat on the saltings. Finding that it had a lead keel, he managed to acquire the boat for almost nothing, removed the keel, and sold this to a scrap metal merchant for far more than the boat cost.

Not content with this profit, he then made a concrete keel to replace the lead one and hopefully offered the yacht for sale. What happened to it, I never found out.

Concrete has its snags. The main one is its lightness compared with iron and lead. The other is that on the boat I was building the after end of the keel narrowed down to only two inches. I was not at all sure whether the concrete would be strong enough to stand any hammering on a hard bottom, or to take the strains of the rudder.

'Why not write to my friend, Robin,' said Michael, my bearded ally and brother-in-law. 'He's a civil engineer, so he knows all about it.' So I wrote to him, giving all the details and telling him the points I was in doubt about. He told me:

'The difficulty about concrete for keels is that salt-water is very corrosive. All iron reinforcement should be covered by at least 2″ of concrete if possible, and ought to be stainless steel, or least galvanized. If ordinary mild steel is used, it is bound to rust eventually and the resulting expansion could crack the concrete in a few months.'*

He advised the use of sulphate-resistant cement to prevent attack on the keel by the magnesium sulphate present in salt-water, and gave details of a very ingenious system for

---

* For Robin's complete instructions see appendix at the end of this book.

arranging for the keel-bolts to be used as reinforcements. These were all things I would not have had the knowledge to think of myself.

I decided to use all stainless steel. This was expensive, but I got it machined fairly cheaply by Brit Engineering, a local Bridport firm. At the same time I got other bolts for joining the large pieces at the stem and stern made of the same material. Stainless steel is the only metal almost totally satisfactory at sea. Its only snag is that it can suffer metal fatigue under stress and become brittle.

The reinforcement was made of ¾" bars and there were bolts every foot. Those I arranged so that they would come up between the floors of the framework at one foot intervals. They would be supported by large cross floors, the lightest being 3" x 3" the heaviest at the stern being a full railway sleeper. These large floors were sawn up out of railway sleepers, out of baulks I bought second hand, or out of driftwood. They were fitted to shape before the planking was put on, but fixed in place later.

The actual bolts were to be fitted into the concrete keel after it was cast. This was for two reasons. In the first place, it is very difficult to arrange the bolts so that they will be in exactly the right place after the concrete has set. Concrete shrinks slightly in setting and in the process of filling up a mould with cement, it is easy to put a bolt out of line, however firmly it is fixed.

The second reason was very ingenious. The bolts had long threads so that nuts could be tightened over steel plates at both top and bottom of the keel. This meant that the concrete would be subject to a prestressing tension to help stop the concrete from cracking under load.

The mould was made up from some of my second-hand tongue and groove before it was used elsewhere on the boat. Removable pieces were made to get the shape of the keel and the mould was built round them, strenthened by old pieces of timber.

Sulphate-resisting cement (used for building on land where agricultural fertilizers have been used), and sand were bought.

Shingle was brought by the sackload from the beach. I was ready to begin. I prepared myself for some hard work. The measurements and mixing had to be exact and it was essential that the concrete should be put into the mould all at once. Cement which is left for more than two hours before being finally placed should not be used. The bolts had been placed in position in the mould and a greased plastic hose placed over them.

All went well until the final two inches. I noticed that under the pressure the mould had started to bulge. Frantically I hunted round for pieces of wood to prop it up. It was impossible to correct the bulging but it seemed to have stopped getting worse. It was difficult to tell since it was now getting dark.

The next morning it was time to remove the mould. When I did so, I could see a distinct bulge down one side. If the keel had bulged on both sides, I might not have worried, but it was plain that the handling of the boat might be affected. So I borrowed a pick from a local builder and hacked the things to pieces. My father had to help me in the end, and even so by the time we had finished the concrete was getting solid. It was very hard work, but at least we had saved the expensive reinforcement for another go.

The second attempt with a stronger mould was much better. The plastic tubes were pulled out, the wooden form removed, and the keel soaked in water several times a day to help curing.

The false keel, the wooden part between the hull and the concrete, had been build while the boat was upside down. It was made out of various odd baulks of timber and glued in place. Getting it to fit into the curve or camber of the bottom took a lot of work. Along the flat top, soon to become the bottom, the positions for the bolt-holes were marked and then drilled through with a gate-post augur, the only thing I could find that was long enough to go through many inches of wood. These holes were then marked on a long strip of wood which was put by for positioning the bolts in the concrete keel. The system worked well.

As the boat progressed, lifting heavy weights became more and more important. The boat, after being built upside down, had to be turned the right way up so that I could work on the deck and cabin. First the mould legs had to be cut away so that the hull was supported at the bow and stern only. The difficulty was what to do then. It was plain that a vast weight would rest on the remaining legs and that this would have to be lowered somehow.

Bearing this vast weight in mind, I cut away the legs carefully. Nothing was likely to happen, of course, but if the boat did fall unexpectedly, any beam I was sitting under at the time would descend with the stunning force of half a ton. As I was sawing away at one of the last legs, the transom supports caved in and the boat dropped with a crash. It solved the problem of how to lower the boat. As I crawled out from under the boat, I saw one of the village youth club standing in the garden witnessing the scene.

'I never thought I'd see you come out of there alive,' he said, grinning casually.

Turning the hull the right way up was a family matter. My father, my brother-in-law Michael, and myself, we all levered one side of the boat up until it was at the point of balance. Then we pushed. It tipped over and bounced on the lawn like a nutshell, making a huge dent in the grass. To my astonishment it did not fall to pieces.

The deck beams had to be faired off with the rest of the hull and the decking added. Glue and sheradised wire nails were used here. Where the cabin top was to be, the full-length beams were sawn off carefully, the pieces to be used later for the cabin-top beams. Cabin-top sides were made, complete with perspex squares built into them to make non-opening portlights. When making the cabin top, glue was not used, in order to save time. This was a mistake.

The most tedious parts of building a boat are the details. Every joint to be fitted takes time. The less skilled one is, the longer it takes. There is hardly a right-angled joint on a boat, each joint varying in two directions, none being the same. When the planking is put on it must all be planed diagonally

ree pictures from
ferent angles of *Erik*
Red 'in frame'. The
at was built upside
wn. First, the four
oulds, the sternpost and
transom mould were
ade up, with legs to
ep them the correct
ight off the ground.
erything had to be
refully measured and
velled up according to
plans. Then the
ingers – beam shelves
d chines – were bent
und the moulds. The
mes and floors had to
fitted on to these, each
e being individually
aped.

e full bulkhead aft and
half bulkhead
ward can be clearly
en. They were made of
inks and stiffened the
at against the strain of
unstayed masts.

e long loose strip on
top of the boat was a
tten for measuring how
uch of the frames and
ors had to be planed
wn so that the planks
uld fit snugly on to
m.

The hull nearly completed apart from the keel. The seams between the planks were caulked with strands of cotton driven in with a special tool. Notice the piece of railway sleeper with a hole in it to take the thrust of the main-mast, and the cabin-top hand rails which double as slides for the hatch. Instead of doors, a square of wood called a wash-board fits into the cabin entrance.
Below : the made-up concrete keel can be seen, with stainless-steel bolts projecting, and damp-course material on top.

to the grain to get a smooth surface to the curve. This is done
at almost impossible angles from an unsupported position.
Planing the bottom of the boat when it was upside down was
a surprisingly difficult task.

With what timber I had left, it was now time to do the
cabin. It was obvious that it would have to be very primitive.
The wood used was very rough with virtually no finish at all.
Everything was painted white down below in order to reflect
the light. The actual living space was about 8 ft. x 5 ft. x
4 ft. 6 ins. The bunks each side of the cabin had partially
removable tops for stowage underneath. By the hatch on one
side was a crudely constructed swinging shelf capable of
taking two paraffin stoves, while on the other were shelves
for stowage facing the bunk. On top of these was a sideboard
at about deck level. Over the galley was a similar removable
shelf, although there was room for cooking to be done
underneath this if necessary.

Under the foredeck and bridge deck was stowage space,
though not very easy to get at. At the far end of the
starboard bunk were two shelves for books. This was all.

By comparison, the cockpit was enormous. The boat was
really designed for day-sailing with a big cockpit. I had a
notion of being able to rig a tent over the cockpit, so I raised
the floor to give an area 6 ft. x 5 ft. It looked very large, and
everyone who saw this cockpit looked doubtfully at it and
said it would fill up at sea. Since it was almost half the boat,
this would be serious.

At the fore-end of the cockpit was a water-tight bulkhead
which entirely split the boat into two compartments, and
formed the after end of the bridge-deck. In a similar manner
there was a half-bulkhead where the main-mast was to be.
These bulkheads were there to support the second obviously-
unusual feature of the boat.

In the original design, the sails were those of a ketch-rig. I
soon worked out that by the time I had paid for the sails,
fittings and rigging, I would be well over my maximum
figure. As it happened, there was a way out. In a copy of the
same magazine I had found details of the boat, *Yachts and*

Yachting, there had been an article about the Chinese rig as used on Chinese junks. I had cut this out and kept it. When I was looking round for a cheap rig, the Chinese one seemed to fit the bill. Also, it looked as if it might be fun to use.

The sails themselves have no shape built into them like a Western sail. They are completely flat, and their shape is entirely controlled by the bamboo battens stretching across the cloth. To make them, I drew a plan on the original sail plan till it looked right, keeping to the original height of the masts. Then I got some cheap unbleached cotton sheeting. The sails were marked out in the attic, the main having to be made in two halves and joined together later. The cloths were laid down and seams put in to support the sail cloth. The sails were then sewn on my mother's sewing machine; it all took the best part of a week.

Bamboos of the right length were bought locally. The Chinese fix these bamboos to the sail with wire, the cloth being sandwiched between the bamboo batten and thinner bamboos on the other side. I did not fancy the idea of using wire so I used twine instead. It was a mistake.

The masts were to be stepped into the deck through strong mast partners. The main mast-partners were a chunk of railway sleeper bolted through the main deck beam. The mast step was a length of railway sleeper with a large square hole cut into it. To stop the mast rotting when rain water dripped down the mast into the mast step, a drain hole had to be bored to let out the water. These little details, like the limber-holes, which drain bilge water from one floor to another are very important at sea.

Both masts were to lean forward considerably, as is traditional in Chinese junks. This is intended to make the sails swing outwards in a light breeze, unlike the Western rig, in which the boom swings inwards and bangs about.

There is no rigging on the masts. This again is traditional in Chinese junks, though many are now stayed to keep up with the times. I had doubts about this system, so I got advice from Lord Strathcona, who had a converted lifeboat motor-sailer using the Chinese rig. He kindly supplied details of the right sizes to use, and suggested that I made the masts hollow. This I was unable to do since I could not get hold of the right timber. I borrowed Skene's *Elements of Yacht Design* from the library, and worked out the sizes for solid masts.

The masts were simply two Douglas fir trees from the New Forest. They were supplied ready barked and cost less than £5 for both. I had a theory that masts should work like fishing rods. If one planed them down thinly at the top, the masts should bend smoothly throughout their length instead of having all the breaking strain just above the deck.

These trees were still green and very knotty. I used an ordinary plane to get them into shape. The foot of each one was planed square to fit into the mast step and stop any twisting. Chocks were screwed to the top to take the halyard strops. As the masts dried out, splits began to appear in them, so I coated them with linseed oil in an attempt to stop the process.

It was now time to finish off the hull. This was treated with Cuprinol as a defence against rot and the teredo worm expected in the tropics. It was then painted with aluminium undercoat ready to be caulked.

The caulking was something I had worried about. I was lucky to have Ernie there to advise me. The local West Bay boatbuilder kindly lent me the two caulking irons needed, and having bought the special cotton I was ready to begin.

The cotton comes in balls made up of cotton strands looking rather like wool. Several of these strands are twisted together and then driven into the seams with the caulking iron and mallet. It looks easy — for an expert. Ernie was very patient.

'You drive in the cotton with this iron here.' He held the one with a thin flat edge. 'That's why this is called a driving iron. Chink in the cotton first, then drive it in, working along.'

He worked with surprising speed along a seam. He showed me the other iron. It had a V-shaped groove along the driving edge.

'This is called your "making iron". This makes a bead along the cotton to hold your putty. When the boat goes into the water, the wood will swell round the cotton and hold it tight. The cotton holds the putty in. There you are. Easy.'

It took me the best part of a week to do the caulking.

Yes, it all takes a long time, boatbuilding.

Day follows upon day, week upon week. How long it is taking! Week after week and then a year has gone by. 'How can it be possible? Is it worth it?', you wonder.

In ordinary life, of course, we may wonder about this too, but then we have so many little but equal things to think of, so great a variety of aims, that the purpose of our actions sinks into a blur of mist.

But when you have just one thing you have set your mind upon, one thing which to the rest of the world seems difficult to understand, then all your doubts and fears take on a single shape and sit upon your plan like a huge rider upon a horse.

Then the journey seems long indeed.

You glance enviously aside under your burden at the pleasant grass-green country you are passing through, and at those who are enjoying it as you too should be enjoying your best and greenest years. All that keeps you going is the belief that this fruit is but a dream and hangs out of reach of those who seem to graze among it.

Or is this wishful thinking by one who does not like to seem envious of others? Of those who do not feel that they must struggle with a task different from the dreams of most of us?

These were the thoughts that passed through my mind as I worked on at the boat, cursing myself for my slowness, my idleness, my inefficiency in not getting this boat built quicker.

It took too long, so long that I was always ashamed to say how long, even when assured by those who knew that to bring a boat to life is sometimes a long, long business.

From first planning to do it, to getting it done, took four years.

Still, maybe when I looked back from an older age, four years would not seem to have been too great a price in priceless time.

When painted, the boat was red. This was because I had bought some cheap paint of the brightest colour I could, and this happened to be red. I could not think of a reasonable name for the boat, so I decided to have the word 'red' in it. Names like *Red Dragon* and *Rudolf the Red-nosed Reindeer* were rejected in favour of *Erik the Red*. Erik the Red was a Viking and the father of Leif Eriksen, who discovered America. On the voyage, I was an instant hit with Scandinavians. Norwegians would come to tell me that Erik the Red was Norwegian, Danes that he was Danish, and Icelanders that he was Icelandic. In fact, he was an Icelandic confidence trickster, exiled for murder, who discovered Greenland. He returned to Iceland, saying that he had discovered a marvellous and fertile land over the sea. This he called Greenland. He was pardoned, and expeditions were sent out to colonize the land. When they got there, they discovered a barren and inhospitable land. Perhaps *Erik the Red* was not the best name for a boat, but I was proud of him.

It was, of course, essential that the boat should be called something unusual. As a joke, I had told everybody who asked the name of the boat I was building that it was a secret until launching. The idea grew up that the name would be extraordinary. In fact, I didn't have the faintest idea what the boat was to be called. If it had turned out to be *Spray*, I would never have lived it down.

It was now time for the mammoth task of getting the boat to the water. After a vain attempt to get hauliers interested, I had decided that the best way to join the keel and the hull, was to take the two parts separately to West Bay Harbour where there was a crane, and fit them together on the quay. With a borrowed trailer and Land Rover, the keel was taken down to the quay, and then the hull itself had to be raised inch by inch onto the trailer, using the masts as sheerlegs, and a chain-hoist. The boat only just went through the gateway.

Down at West Bay, the hull was lifted onto the keel, with

damp-course material between the two to make a good fit. The bolts were tightened down. All that was needed now was for the surplus deadwood to be removed so that it was flush with the keel and this was done with an axe and a plane. The rudder was attached to bolts embedded into the concrete keel, and the bottom was painted, finished off with anti-fouling. All this took a week. Then *Erik the Red* was ready for launching. It was just before Christmas Day, 1969.

When he went into the water, I discovered that I was amazed to see him floating. This was not quite the right attitude. It would take more than just floating to get us across the Atlantic.

5. Trial

It is remarkable that West Bay harbour is there at all. It is built at the Western end of the notorious Chesil Beach, a part of the Dorset coast which looks beautiful on a sunny day but in on-shore gales becomes a death-trap. Portland Bill with its dangerous tide-race is to the south-east, and many a ship unable to weather the Bill has foundered in a southerly gale. Sailors who tried to swim ashore were carried out again by the vicious undertow to drown in the surf.

The harbour is officially known as Bridport and is made of two piers which jut out into the sea to form a gap between the banks of shingle. The entrance is long and narrow, and in a storm the waves roll all the way up it to affect even those boats at the far end of the basin beyond.

Opposite the entrance, the waters of the River Brit are pent up by sluice gates. These are opened at low tide and the water rushes out to wash the channel clear of shingle.

At low tides the harbour dries out, except for one part of the inner end of the channel. This was where *Erik the Red* had to lie.

Small coastal freighters sometimes come into the harbour at high tides and dry out by the quay to unload timber and take on shingle. They usually lay where *Erik the Red* now was. As this was just before Christmas, no ship was expected for some weeks. Since the passage between the piers is so narrow, a large ship finds it tricky to enter, and in bad weather, which can normally be expected in winter, might get into difficulties. The old sailing coasters used to be towed in by men walking along a raised plank-walk, the remains of which can still be seen. Sometimes they put a sail up to help them. Sometimes the skipper would lower sail outside the harbour, letting the vessel come up through the piers under its own momentum to stop at exactly the right place.

When the boat was lying by the quay, I chose the time of low tide to put the masts in. My brother Neil helped with this. Since there are no shrouds on the masts, manoeuvering them into position in the mast-steps is rather like tossing the caber. With a bit of juggling, we managed it.

The sails then had to be put on, and since the rig was unfamiliar to me, this took a lot of time. Apart from what I had learnt, all the details and strengths of the materials had to be guessed at. Everyone who saw the sails said they would blow to pieces. But the only fisherman whose opinion I valued looked at the boat and said:

'You could go round the world in that — if the worms don't get you first.'

This was cheering.

Although I had tried to keep the whole project private, the local paper, the *Bridport News* had come to hear about it. Bowing to the inevitable, I gave the reporter all the details, and invited him to come for a trip.

'I've got to take the boat out of the harbour,' I told him confidently, 'to see how it handles. You'll be very useful. And think what a scoop it would be for you.'

He looked doubtful but agreed to come.

The sailing day was bright and clear, and cold with a winter Easterly blowing. A beam wind both out of and into the harbour! It could not be any better.

After a final check of the gear, I gave orders to cast off. With willing hands those standing above obeyed, then they gathered to watch the fun. As soon as *Erik the Red* began to drift towards the middle of the harbour, as if by magic a great row of fishermen and other lay-abouts began to line the quay.

Trying to ignore this audience, I managed to get the sails up, then took over the tiller. We started to sail majestically the wrong way, towards the sluice. It was plain we would have to tack.

When I put the helm down, however, the boat refused to go about. We were not going fast enough and I had not learnt yet that putting a Chinese-rigged boat about can be almost like tacking a square-rigger. Fortunately I had prepared for this eventuality. I had lashed to each side of the cockpit a dinghy oar in such a way that it might be possible to row with them. The arrangement was very unsatisfactory. My crew could not know this, and thought that any difficulties were due to his inexperience.

I pointed to the port hand oar.

'Row!' I ordered in my best Captain Bligh manner.

My crew struggled manfully with the oar. I could see at once that it was an impossible task .... But he achieved the impossible! Round we came and headed out between the piers.

In my caution, I had not hoisted all of the large sail area. This had two results. In the first place, it meant that the sheets for hauling in the sails turned out to be longer than they should have been. Secondly, it meant that all of the sail area was low down.

When we came in between the piers, the wind was shadowed by them so that only the top part of each sail was effective. The swell we now met coming in between the piers threatened to shake what little wind we had from the sails. And to make matters worse, the wind came round towards the bow, forcing us to be close-hauled. But the sheets were too long to pull the sails in.

We edged towards the Western pier. The bow hit a pile with a splintering crash, and the boat came side-ways on with the sails dragging along the wall. We tried to push off from the pier with oars, but we were going up and down several feet in the swell, which dislodged our grip. We were stuck against that wall like a fly in wet paint.

'Keep us off the wall,' I swinishly ordered my gallant crew, and quickly started to disentangle a warp to throw to the other side. This was now so crowded with the spectators of this fiasco that I am surprised it did not sink into the sea under the weight.

After a few unsuccessful throws, the light polypropylene line blowing back in the wind, someone managed to catch the warp and we were towed off the wall. Out between the piers we went and to sea.

It was quite choppy outside and the wind was obviously increasing. There was not much time for sailing before I thought we had better go in again. The tide was now on the ebb, and this could start to make re-entry difficult.

There was no difficulty about coming in. Learning from my mistake before I had a line ready for throwing and we were towed along the channel to our berth. Fiasco it had been perhaps. The fairlead platform had been torn away and was held on by one bolt. I could hardly claim to have been in control of the situation.

But I had learnt something. *Erik the Red* was all right. She handled under sail, that brief trial out at sea had shown that. The helm felt right. And whatever the defects of the sails, the rig had taken a hammering against the quay which would have splintered anything other than its flexible bamboos, and have demolished the rigging of a modern yacht caught against such a quay.

My brave crew, the reporter, got off the boat quicker than he got on, for which I do not blame him. But for myself, I had the feeling that the boat might not turn out such a disaster as I had first thought.

Now that I had a boat and she was in the water, I was committed to leaving England at least. 'I'm going south,' I used to say grandly. Meanwhile I got on with my preparations for a voyage. My idea was to sail down the Channel. If things went swimmingly, then I would head off across Biscay. But this would only be if there was a northerly wind which looked likely to set in for some time. Otherwise, I would put into Brixham or, if possible, Falmouth.

At any rate, it was plain that I should have to leave as soon as possible. Since that first little trial the weather had been consistently bad. Also, no one had warned me about the sluice.

The piling around the quays of West Bay harbour is not

ideal for a small boat. The space between each vertical timber
is so wide that it is almost impossible to fend a boat off
properly. I used long lengths of wood lashed to car tyres to
keep the boat away. I was therefore amazed to discover one
day that the rubbing-strake had been ripped off. I found out
the reason at low tide.

At spring tides when the tides are very low, the water level
sinks well below the vertical piling of the quay, revealing a
horizontal baulk. There is nothing to prevent the low sides of
a boat getting underneath this. When the sluices were opened,
the water would pour out in a mad stream, reaching speeds of
perhaps ten knots. The water level rose quickly. It is easy to
imagine what would happen to a boat caught under the piling
at this time.

The only cure for this was for me to be sitting on the boat
when the sluices were opened ready for fending off. The
force of water was incredible.

Meanwhile I had stowed away my stores of food, and
water and paraffin. For food I simply went to a 'cash and
carry' and bought as much as I could that was cheap. It
seemed to be mostly porridge.

A series of January gales set in. The waves at high tide
would roll along between the piers and catch the boat,
making him surge back and forward on his warps like a toy.
The only thing was to keep the boat away from the quay in
these circumstances, to run a line across the harbour to one of
the mooring buoys and lash it round the main mast.

The boat was lying with his stern towards the sea, since he
would have sunk if he had not taken the water of the sluice
bows on. Thus when a gale blew up the waves would roll in
and catch him on the stern. Often his warps were doubled,
trebled, and these treble warps doubled — and still the lines
parted. I got into the habit of driving down to the quay at
high spring tides when there was a wind and just sitting there
to be ready for anything that might happen. Usually this was
in the middle of the night.

One accident and the boat might be wrecked. If he came
adrift nothing could save him from a great deal of damage. In

spite of all my precautions, the repaired rubbing strake had been demolished again. I made ready to leave the harbour at the first opportunity. Anything would be better than keeping the boat by this quay. Bridport harbour is not uniquely bad in this respect. Quays are designed for large work-boats. One of the rules I learnt later was never to lie alongside a quay if it could possibly be avoided.

A gentle north wind was blowing. In spite of it being February, the weather seemed set fair. I had on board my stores, my charts, thick clothing. Everything was very primitive, but I thought that I had all I could possibly need. The sails had been adjusted so that as far as I could tell, they were working perfectly. It was now afternoon and time to be off. In winter, night comes early.

I said goodbye to my parents, and the sails were partially hoisted, enough to take advantage of a fair wind straight out of the harbour, and I cast off.

It was a strange feeling to sail out of the harbour, thinking, 'This is it.' It was a feeling of astonishment, and disbelief. Some of those watching said later that they had never expected to see me again.

Once out of the harbour, I hoisted all sail. I had worked out my compass course long before, and set off towards Start Point. It began to get dark and the bright frosty stars appeared. Soon the shore-line had vanished. Bridport was now just a mysterious glow of light astern with tiny sparks above coming from solitary houses on the hills. The glows of Lyme and Seaton also kept me brief company, then I was alone, sailing through the darkness.

The gentle breeze blew steadily on and on. The sea, under the shelter of the land was calm, though gradually grew rougher as we made an offing. After a while I hove-to and lit the Tilley lamp to look at the chart. If I was going to turn into Brixham, it would soon be best to do so. As it was time for the weather forecast, I turned on my little radio. For some inexplicable reason it refused to work. I took off the back and examined it, I shook it and banged it. Nothing happened. Still, I thought, I don't need a weather forecast.

It's obviously going to stay fine for a couple of days. It's perfect for going into Falmouth. So I kept on to Start Point.

Soon I saw its light flashing. We were making a good speed with the wind so favourable. Start Point grew closer and closer and by dawn we were four or five miles off land, with Start Point bearing north.

With the dawn, the wind dropped completely, and we were left helplessly rolling in the swell. It was a beautifully sunny winter's day at sea. I could see land clearly. I wished that I had an engine.

At dusk Start Point light began to flash and a southerly breeze got up. It freshened and veered to the south-west. The light got closer and closer, and it was plain that we were being carried towards Start Point. Regretfully I decided to put about on the other tack. The wind got stronger and stronger, and I lowered sail until there was nothing left. The wind was now gale force.

A succession of gales now set in, mostly from the westward. This was not an easy time. Gales are never pleasant and in winter tend to be more severe and frequent than in summer.

The first thing was to make sure that I was on the right tack. In a gale it is nearly always safer to keep out at sea rather than to try and make port, especially if your boat has ·no engine and is not very manoeuvrable.

I found that when hove-to, or drifting without sails up, we would make from one to two knots down wind depending upon the strength of the gale and from a half to one knot towards the direction in which the boat was heading. In a very prolonged gale it would be possible to come close to the French coast. So, if there is any reason to expect a gale from a northerly direction, this too, could be dangerous. Besides, my aim was to put into port if possible. An English port would be easier than a French one, since I did not have any charts of the French coast.

These were the thoughts which prompted me to keep out from the coast, but not too far out of reach. I was aware that a small boat in a gale could easily get trapped in Lyme Bay.

Now that it was too late for it to do any good, my little
radio sprang back into life again to give its gloomy forecasts.
A southerly gale set in with drizzle. Rain swept across the
sea, until I could see nothing but the boat as it lifted to each
crested wave. It began to get dark.

My pressure lamp lit perfectly but it was no match for the
onslaught of that wind. I had to tie pieces of cloth round the
bottom to try and stop the mantle blowing out. These are
occasions when electric lights seem essential. This lamp
however, when it was going, gave out as much light as an
electric one and in fact no light could make much difference
in the murk.

Once I thought I heard a thumping noise above the roar of
the sea and looked out. Not twenty feet away, the side of a
ship, rolling and pitching madly, slid past, the lights from its
ports making a dim impression in the haze. They did not see
us.

I was now somewhere in the centre of Lyme Bay. When it
was light, I could see no sign of land. There was no way of
finding out where I was. Then a ship came into sight, saw us,
hove to, and circled round. I waved. They hooted two short
blasts and a long one. This is the letter U, which in the
Maritime Code means, 'you are standing into danger'. I put
Erik the Red on the other tack so that I was heading out to
sea and they went away. Perhaps they knew that we were
nearer to the land than I had thought.

The forecast was bad, gale force eight or nine. Sure enough
it was soon blowing harder than ever. It was now very cold.
How I survived that cold I shall never know. I had brought
along a collection of ancient jerseys from which I had cut the
arms so that it would be possible to wear half a dozen at the
same time like a waistcoat, yet still be able to move my arms.
These were a great standby. All I could do at this time was to
lie on my bunk trying to keep warm.

The effort of just boiling water to make tea or coffee was
tremendous. Mostly I lived on digestive biscuits or fruit,
when it was really rough. As I lay in my bunk that night
trying to keep warm, I listened to the radio forecast. I could

hardly believe it. 'Storm force ten, eleven locally,' it said. I thought, 'This is it. Now I've had it.'

The wind increased, until nothing could be seen but huge white topped waves rushing towards us in the darkness. After that ship's warning, I had put a small bit of the mizen sail up, hoping that this would push us out from the coast. Somewhere under our lee was Portland, possibly close but unseen in the bad visibility.

Abruptly the wind changed, veering round to the north. The sea became chaotic, with the wind driving across the waves.

All this time *Erik the Red* behaved magnificently. Every time a wave struck him, it would break underneath the bottom, lifting him up into the air. Sometimes a 'howler' would come our way. One of these waves let out something between a whistle and a roar, and sounded menacingly evil. It would strike the boat, which, because of the force of the wind on his masts, would be lying over with the lee deck half under water. Torrents of water would pour down the bridge-deck, half of it finding its way over the sill and into the cockpit.

These low sills worried me and I began to devise ways of nailing on higher pieces. Eventually, though, I realized that it was easier just to pump it out, since the quantity, though large, was not dangerous.

I thought, 'I shall never face anything as bad as this again'. The gale subsided to a mere force eight and Portland light came into view to the eastward. I headed for it. The best plan now seemed to be to make into Weymouth harbour in the lee of Portland. Portland Bill's dangerous race extends four miles off shore so it was essential to keep well outside. Small boats have been sunk by this tidal race which is caused by the tides sweeping round the Bill over an uneven bottom.

When I headed in towards Weymouth harbour, the whole area had been kicked up by wind and tide into a seething mass. It was plain that one could easily lose control in there and be carried into the race. Looking at the chart, the obvious answer was Poole harbour. This is a fairly easy harbour to enter, since it is sheltered by Studland Point. Once under the lee of the point I would be safe.

At this moment, the Navy took a hand in the affair. A vessel festooned with red lights, approached in the dusk and started to harass me whenever I set off towards Poole. East of Portland is a gunnery range which the Navy keep to themselves by loosing off guns at intervals. Coupled with a change of wind which now made it possible to head down Channel again, this decided me to stick to my original plan and try to make Falmouth. At least we would then have got some of the way, instead of going backwards.

Half-way to Start Point we encountered another westerly gale but it seemed mild in comparison with the last one. I was beginning to worry now about a shortage of paraffin. In the tremendous beating we had taken, half the plastic paraffin containers had somehow unscrewed their tops and emptied themselves into the bilges. The foul smell was very off-putting. Paraffin seemed to have soaked into all the wood-work.

Off Start Point both sails suddenly fell down in quick succession. Fortunately the wind dropped to a calm soon after. But even in a calm it is not easy to climb a mast. I had no rigging upon which I might have rigged ratlines, nor was I able to haul myself up. In the swell, climbing the masts proved impossible.

What had happened, I discovered, was that I had not made the halyard strops strong enough. These hold up the halyard blocks at the top of the mast, but they had chafed and broken. After much thought and several false tries, I managed to hoist strops up the mast as high as I could get them, using the lifts which held up the bottom of the sails. These strops were arranged so that a jerk on a piece of string jammed them up immovably. After several hours' work the sails were in business again, though they were much reduced in area.

Slowly and painfully we limped along trying to make Falmouth. I had by this time, mastered enough of my navigation to be able to get a latitude. How far along the coast we were, I could not tell, but I knew that if we kept

Erik the Red, completed apart from the keel, being lifted up so that a trailer can be pushed underneath. The tripod is made up from the two masts and the village maypole which happened to be knocking about at the time. A chain-hoist was borrowed from the local garage and each end of the boat raised in turn.

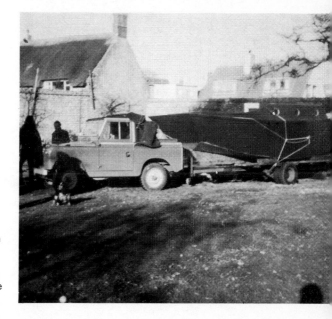

Erik the Red, without keel, ready to go. The trailer only just went through the stone gateway of my father's Rectory garden.

The keel was taken down to West Bay Harbour separately, and the hull lifted on to it by crane. It was a good thing that the keel bolts fitted into the holes already drilled through the wooden keel of the boat. This wooden keel was planed off to match the concrete one. The rudder too could now be fitted on to the boat, and the bottom painted with anti-fouling paint.

Erik the Red aground for painting in Spain. He was leaned first one way and then the other. The unstayed masts can be clearly seen, also the lifts which held up the furled sails. Notice the frame-work for the canvas-covered cockpit shelter, later abandoned. The police here at Sancti Petri were not very pleased to see us.

exactly west, we would come into sight of the Lizard.

It seems amazing now, but these events which have been described in not many words filled many days. Where did the time go to? What did I do? Perhaps I shall never remember. But for one thing, I used to listen to the radio quite a lot while resting in the cabin, and on the eighth day I was listening to the News. Suddenly I jerked to attention.

'A red yacht has been sighted drifting without anyone on board, south-west of the Eddystone Lighthouse. An air-sea search has been started.'

Whether this referred to us, I did not know, but I knew my parents would be worried by this report. I should have to get to Falmouth as soon as possible. That day I was lying a-hull, resting until I was ready to set out again on course. I heard a plane roar over-head, and looked out of the hatch. A four-engined plane was turning and now roaring back. Several objects fell out of it into the sea. They were smoke flares. One caught alight, while the others sank without trace.

The plane zoomed around while I waved to show that I was still alive. Then it went away. The wind had dropped by now and there was a providential breeze from the south. I still delayed in case the plane had been in touch with some ship which was now speeding in my direction. Nothing happened however, and night fell. I put the boat on a westerly course.

Towards the end of the night I was becoming anxious because I had seen no sign of the Lizard light. Then I saw it. I could hardly believe my luck. I turned *Erik the Red* towards it, and took a careful note of the bearing. All that next day I sat at the helm. The wind was light, but still from the south, and I was determined to stay at the helm until I had made Falmouth.

There was no sign of land until night fell again, then the Lizard light showed clearly ahead. By next morning I was heading in towards Falmouth harbour. As we passed Black Rock buoy, the Customs boat came out towards us.

'Have you got any dutiable stores aboard?' they shouted. I did not take this question kindly since I had been refused permission to take any duty-free stores. The boat was too small, they had said.

Still they offered me a tow which I gladly accepted, since the wind had dropped. It seemed that this trip had been even more of a fiasco than the first one. Unbelievably, we had been out there for ten long, long days.

6. Start again

The Press, in the form of a freelance reporter, was waiting for me. He gave me a filmed interview on the boat and then took me off for a clean-up and a meal whilst *Erik the Red* was left moored at Falmouth Town Quay. Publicity is difficult to avoid when you do not want it.

I made enquiries about where I could leave the boat while I did repairs to the rig. This had become frayed somewhat in the storm off Portland. From the part of the mizen which had been up in the gale, the seam of the after edge of the sail had been completely blown away. The halyards, too, would have to be re-rigged.

Fortunately, an elderly couple who used to live in our village, and now lived near Falmouth, came to see me and made arrangements for me to see a friend of theirs, leaving *Erik the Red* in Porth Navas creek up the Helford River. Mr Hodges was in charge of the Helford oyster fisheries. In spite of his seemingly stern appearance, with his ice-cold blue eyes, he kindly lent me his own mooring until I should be ready to go again. The next day, I took the boat up the Helford River and left him there, catching a bus back home to gather my wits.

The harbour master at Falmouth had advised me not to go until about May.

'I know nothing about it,' he tactfully said. 'I used to sail on the Indian Line, so I know nothing about the Atlantic at all. But if I were you, I'd wait until May and then sail down to the Mediterranean. You can look around there, and then it'll be fine to sail to Las Palmas in the autumn.'

What he said made good sense. It would give me time to do repairs on the boat and to make good of the preparations I had neglected. I would also have a rest for a while. . . .

A few days after I had come home, a yacht deliverer called Jim, who lives locally, rang me up. I had been to visit him to discuss my prospective trip to the West Indies. He was a shortish, stout man, with a dashing goatee beard.

'Would you like to come and help me do a yacht delivery? There'll be three of us going. This is a salvage job for Lloyds. The yacht's at Lorient in France.'

In spite of the fact that I was supposed to be recovering from my last trip, I jumped at the chance. It sounded interesting, and would be some money earned. I borrowed some oilskins and we set off to Lorient by train.

'I know nothing about the boat,' Jim told us, 'but Lloyd's have an agent there, who says the boat's seaworthy.'

Lorient is a large port on the coast of Brittany. When we arrived, it was morning. We had arranged to meet the Lloyd's agent at the main hotel. He was nowhere to be found. Then we made enquiries about where the 'Yacht Anglais' was moored. No-one had heard of such a thing. We looked in all the yacht basins. None of the yachts filled the description we had been given. We had to wait until the next day to find the agent and the yacht.

The yacht was propped up on the quayside. Jim decided that it was not ready for sea, since there was a gaping hole in the rudder. He had this repaired, and we got in supplies for the trip to Gosport near Southampton, where the yacht had to be taken.

She was a sailing yacht of some thirty feet. She had been found by fishermen in the Bay of Biscay half-full of water. It was discovered that the toilet, which worked by pumping its contents into the sea, had started to let water into the boat. In the turmoil, the owner had gone overboard and been lost, and the crew had taken to the life-raft. He came ashore safely.

Sailing a yacht with a death to its credit across the Channel in mid-winter did not seem the best of prospects. The yacht was launched by crane and we made everything ready as best we could. We inspected the rigging and sails. Mike, who owned a garage, looked after the engine. Then we set off.

It was extremely cold, but the weather was mild. We made good progress through the Raz de Sein and headed towards Ushant. In bad weather this rocky coast with its strong tides is a very dangerous one. It pays to have an engine. The engine, however, despite our mechanic, refused to work, and we had to put into Brest. Here we got some diesel mechanics in, and they found that the mechanics in Lorient had not put the head gasket on properly.

We had had a hard fight in and out of Brest. We did this twice before the engine was satisfactory. This took time and our mechanic decided he would have to go back to his garage. There were now just the two of us.

It was still bitterly cold, but the weather was settled. We took advantage of the tide to go straight through the Chenal du Four, between the Isle of Ushant and the mainland. At springs, the tides can run at over six knots here. The engine we kept going, since we wanted to get through as quickly as possible. It was a one cylinder diesel and at every stroke, the boat shook with the explosion. It was like sailing a pneumatic drill.

The wind was northerly and fresh. It is a curious fact that ever since I came into Falmouth after fighting westerly gales, the wind had been northerly. This went on for a month, and was perfect for a trip down to Spain. Now I was a long way from my boat, and going in the wrong direction.

It was cold, very cold. Being a modern yacht and having had her self-steering vane broken, there was no way in which she would steer herself. One of us had to be in the cockpit and at the helm all the time. If any sail changing was needed, the one below was called.

Two hours was as much as one could stand in that biting wind, and this did not give the watch below much time for rest. One of us would come off watch with frozen hands and feet, then go below to make something hot to drink on the spirit stove. It took a long while to boil water. Then it was time to lie on a bunk wrapped in sleeping-bags trying to get warm enough to sleep. This happened about half an hour before the end of the watch, when it was time to go on deck again. Sometimes the call came before that to do some sail-changing.

The wind was always north, but the yacht drove into it beautifully, going fast. Then, half-way across the Channel, the bilge water rose above the floorboards in the cabin. Not only water, but something else as well. . . .

When the French shipwrights had been repairing the toilet which had given all the trouble before, they had simply removed all the refuse into the bilges, blocking up the limber holes so that the pump would not clear the water. It also made an undesirable foetid smell, as it slopped all over the cabin with the motion of the boat.

All this stuff had to be bailed out by hand by the one who was resting below. We tried fishing up to our elbows in it to get at the pump, but it was no good. The water still came in from somewhere. Jim made sure that the inflatable life raft was ready for immediate use and told me to get a container of water ready to put into it. I am glad to say that it was not needed. As the wind dropped a little, the water came in more slowly.

'I expect the boat's been strained,' Jim explained to me. 'She's been raced hard for a couple of years, and now when she's driven hard on the wind, the garboards open up. This boat was supposed to be sea-worthy. I'll certainly give Lloyd's a rocket when I get back.'

He did. Very creditably, they thanked him for doing so.

We approached Portland Bill just before dawn. There were a few flakes of snow falling. It was very strange to see Portland Bill again after my last experience of it. Now, as we approached it after our ordeal, Portland harbour looked very inviting. Jim had decided to put in there.

'When we get ashore,' Jim said, 'I'm going to get us the best meal I can.'

The sky lightened and the sea looked smooth and inviting. Jim looked at me sidelong.

'You know,' he said thoughtfully, 'with the wind like this, it wouldn't have taken us long to get to the Solent. It couldn't have been better.'

'It seems a pity to waste it,' I agreed.

We laughed at each other, knowing that we would carry on to Gosport.

In fact, the voyage to Gosport was delightful. Though cold, the weather was sunny and light. The Solent itself was almost deserted. We came into Camper and Nicholson's yard where the yacht was to be left, and Jim told them to keep pumping. As we were talking, an American came by, and Jim introduced himself as a yacht deliverer. He went off to arrange a job to pilot the American's yacht across the Bay of Biscay. He was a glutton for punishment. Then we went home.

A few days later, he rang me up.

'You remember that American yacht at Gosport? It's turned into a delivery job. The owner has appendicitis and has to have an operation. He wants me to take it to Gibraltar. Would you like to come?'

We agreed on terms and off we went to Gosport.

Two friends of the owner, a young American couple, were to go with us. We saw very little of her, since she retired to her cabin, sea-sick throughout the trip. For the other three of us, the trip turned out fairly well. The wind was almost permanently north-easterly and never rose above force six, but it was very cold, all the way down to Spain.

The boat had a good engine, and we used this in the calms. It took only ten days to get round to Gibraltar. We never had a hard wind.

Both these trips I found very valuable experience. Although there is no way to learn navigation other than doing it yourself, it is certainly worth seeing what goes on in a boat run by an experienced skipper. I was able to review my equipment and see how my boat compared with the others. He did not compare well.

In the first place, he had no engine. These are unnecessary incumbrances out at sea, but near land they are very useful.

But, apart from the fact that I could not afford an engine, I had a grand idea that sailing should be done without one. To sail without an engine is perfectly all right if your boat has a modern handy rig with plenty of light canvas. The rig I was using, however, was far from modern and handy.

My navigational equipment, too, was somewhat primitive. For a compass, I had an old box type complete with proper compass points instead of new-fangled degrees on its compass-card. Its green brass fittings had never seen brass polish, but it was duly admired wherever I went.

I also had an old R.A.F. grid steering compass which I had picked up for a few shillings when a boy, because it was cheap. I never used it.

For taking bearings of land objects in order to fix a position, most people have a hand-held compass with special sights. I had no such thing, nor did I need one. If I happened to be compelled to do such a complicated piece of navigation, I used the main compass.

A sextant can be a very expensive piece of equipment. I could not afford to buy one made of brass in the traditional way. I bought a plastic one costing five guineas, and I tried it out with a latitude sight on the beach at home before I left. The beach seemed to be where the map said it should be. On the other hand, I could not be sure that I was not juggling my figures to fit in with where I knew myself to be.

To take sights with a sextant, it is necessary to have a Nautical Almanack of the correct year. I used *Reed's Almanack*, which had the advantage of giving a great deal of other information as well. Finding one's latitude from the position of the sun at noon is not very difficult.

Longitudes are a different matter. I searched round for ages to find a book which described how to get a longitude position without knowing the exact time, but could not find one. Therefore, I should have to have something to give the exact time.

Chronometers are very expensive and were definitely out of the question. I compromised on a very cheap water-proof watch and the ordinary transistor radio which I had already.

This would receive ordinary broadcasting stations on Long and Medium wave bands. I did not realize at the time that not many countries use the Long wave band. One valuable aid which it is possible to use with an ordinary radio is the position fixing method called 'Consol'. This is a series of dots and dashes, and with the right sort of table or chart, one can find the bearing of the transmitting station. It has a range of a thousand miles, but there are not many stations.

Charts are expensive, and I had to economize on them. I bought the Admiralty Pilots for the areas I intended to go to. I hoped these would tell me which parts were dangerous to enter without charts. I had a chart of the Atlantic, a chart covering England to the Canaries and Azores, two charts of the English Channel, one of the Straits of Gibraltar, and one of that part of the West Indies where I might be likely to come to land. These pilots and charts I was given by friends in our village.

I was also given a solid fuel emergency stove, and packets of dehydrated food. Such kindness came from people who were more far-sighted than I was.

I still had my stores which I found in good condition when I went down to Cornwall to stock up and to prepare *Erik the Red*. He was still in a mess after his trial trip. Bedding and clothes had to be dried out, which was not easy since it was only March.

Moored next to me in the creek was a ketch belonging to a character called Paul Johnson. I found later that he was very well-known in the Caribbean, having sailed a 16-foot Shetland fishing vessel with a cabin built on, across the Atlantic. He was another person who gave me very useful advice.

I made all the necessary repairs to the sails. I discovered now that my idea of using twine to fasten the bamboo battens to the sails was a bad one. It was impossible to make this tight enough to stop the battens moving about on the cloth, and once this happened, the twine chafed through. So when doing these repairs, I decided to stick to the Chinese method of using a couple of turns of wire and twisting the ends with a pair of pliers. The clipped off ends were pushed underneath a bamboo.

To re-rig the halyards, the sails were hoisted. Using the parrel lines fixed to the battens, I could then climb up the mast like a ladder, carrying new strops with halyards attached. Profiting by my last experience, I took the precaution of rigging spare halyards. There were no spare sails. Although the sails had suffered some damage, all of it was minor. I was very encouraged by the way the sails had stood up to their first test. There did not seem to be anything now that could happen to the sails that I could not repair in some way at sea.

The masts, too, had stood up. Of course, all my calculations had shown that they would, but there was nothing more convincing than seeing them still there.

All in all, I was confident that the boat could do a long voyage. After all, people had criticized the keel saying that it would drop off, and that it was too light to give the boat stability. That the cockpit was too big, and would fill with water. Also, that it was foolish to go to sea without an engine or a radio, or even a self-inflating life-raft.

The dangers I was now most worried about were those which depended upon myself — being run down by a ship, and running ashore. Nowadays, there is a great deal of shipping in the Channel and along other shipping lanes. I had done enough sailing at sea to know how much there is. There is almost no danger if you can keep a proper watch and not rely on the other ship to see you. For a single-hander, this means staying awake at night or carrying a light bright enough to be easily spotted by anyone. The official yacht lights are not like this. Therefore, I decided to carry only my paraffin pressure lamp, which gives out a very bright white light.

The worst condition for a single-hander is fog. It is one of the rules of the sea that the captain of a vessel must always be on the bridge in fog. In the same way, a single-hander should be on watch all the time in case he should miss the hoot of a ship. To prepare myself for this, I got some amphetamine sulphate pills from the doctor and put them in the medicine box. I hoped that I should not have to use them.

The only other safety equipment I carried, consisted of some hand-held flares, red and white. These, too, I hoped I should never have to use.

My little rubber dinghy was too small to be of any real use for carrying myself, let alone carrying stores, and altogether too dampening. I borrowed a dinghy from the Porth Navas boat builder to carry stuff across. Soon everything I could think of, or at least everything I felt I could afford, was ready. By the beginning of May, there was no real excuse for delaying further.

The gear I had on board sounded enough, though the whole project seemed to depend too much on the original shoestring. I estimated the costs as follows:—

BOAT	Plans, tools, masts, sails, rigging, timber, glue, fastenings, concrete keel.	£165
GEAR	Anchors, chain, dinghy, paints (for whole voyage), other gear.	£60
NAVIGATIONAL GEAR		£30
STORES	Some in bulk to last up to six months.	£50

In addition, I had fifty pounds in traveller's cheques. This was to be my reserve, never to be spent if possible, In cash, I had twenty pounds. After all, I thought, I would not need more than this. My plan was to get a job in Gibraltar.

7. To Gibraltar

In the morning of the 10th May we left Porth Navas Creek for the mouth of the Helford River. The next morning we were still at this mouth of the Helford River. It was flat calm and I had decided to drop anchor for the night. It was not a good start.

I was, I remember, feeling rather nervous. There was nowhere further on to go than Falmouth, so I could not put in anywhere else in England and say that I was just on the way. It was Spain, or bust.

That morning was foggy. By late afternoon the fog had lifted and a beautiful little wind came out of the north. We were on our way. I now experimented with getting the boat to steer himself.

I had discovered that the boat would steer himself closehauled if I lashed the helm amidships. With the wind aft, however, this would not work. *Erik* would gradually swing round and point up into the wind, or else, if I lashed the helm to counteract this, he would creep round the other way and gybe. In a strong wind, this is not recommended.

I had thought about this self-steering business. It seemed to me that I had a big advantage in not having stays on my masts. It meant that I could let off the sheets as far as I liked, even until the sails were pointing straight forward. I tried this now with the mizen, pulled it in a bit so that it was catching some wind, and lashed the sheet to the tiller. To the other side of the tiller I had some shock-cord fastened to the eyebolt on the starboard side. It needed several lengths to counteract the pull of the sheet.

Then with the boat on a south-westerly course, I adjusted the sheet and the shock-cord until they were exactly balanced, and stood back.

The wind was on the quarter, northerly, and a steady force three. Since most of the wind was uselessly spilled out of the mizen, we were not doing better than three knots. But we were going, and the boat was steering himself! I was flabbergasted that I should have solved the self-steering problem so easily and had a celebration drink from my only bottle of brandy. Luckily I did not know that I had by no means solved the problem yet.

The first night I had decided to stay awake. We were still not far from the Lizard, and from looking at the chart and trying to guess the routes that big ships would take, I thought there might be a lot of shipping about here.

Leaving the land is almost as exciting as coming towards it. I could see the Lizard winking at me hypnotically, like a yellow eye, gradually going further and further away. The night was chilly, since this was only May, but after *Erik the Red*'s last voyage it seemed almost warm. Two ships passed that night, but it was not necessary to take avoiding action.

At dawn, I went to my bunk, heavy-eyed after the long night, to be woken a little while later by a fishing-boat hailing to see if I was all right. I waved and they went away. The wind had dropped, and the visibility was poor. These conditions lasted another day.

Being becalmed in bad visibility where there is likely to be shipping about is one of the more dangerous things that a boat without an engine can do. You are completely helpless to get out of the way, and in fog it is essential to make your presence known to any ships. I had no hooter, nor had I bothered about one, finding that if I banged on a tin tray I had, it made a noise fit to wake the dead.

Many ships relied on radar to give them warning of any obstacles. In theory, I was told, it is possible for a good radar operator to pick up a sea-gull on the water several hundred feet away. But this requires continuous attention to the radar set, and most ships' captains are not concerned with sea-gulls.

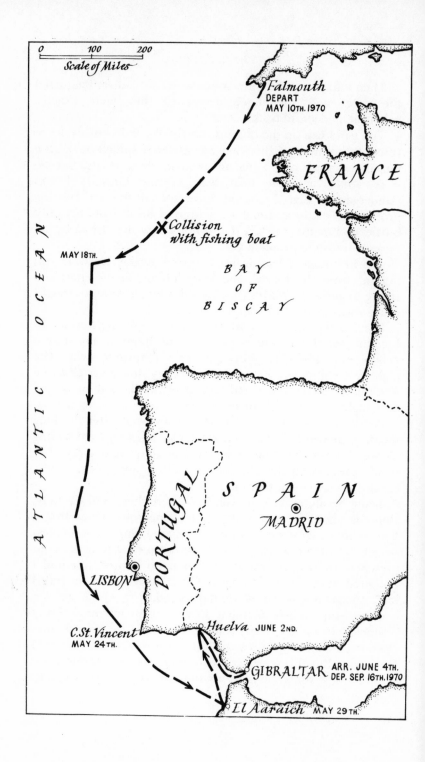

Scale of Miles

0   100   200

Falmouth
DEPART
MAY 10TH. 1970

FRANCE

Collision
with fishing boat

MAY 18TH.

BAY
OF
BISCAY

ATLANTIC OCEAN

PORTUGAL

SPAIN

MADRID

LISBON

C. St. Vincent
MAY 24TH.

Huelva JUNE 2ND.

GIBRALTAR ARR. JUNE 4TH.
DEP. SEP. 16TH.1970

El Aaraich MAY 29TH.

Therefore they turn their sets to minimum sensitivity, so that it will not need constant adjustment. This gives them warning of any obstacle likely to cause them danger. Even so, big ships still collide in fog, radar or not.

A small wooden yacht gives out a very feeble echo. For this reason, most yachts and fishing boats carry a radar reflector to increase the echo. Before I left, I had been told by a friend who was a radio expert to hoist a biscuit tin to the top of the mast. This, he said, cost nothing, and was as good as a radio reflector.

This I did. The trouble was, instead of being proud of my biscuit tin as I should have been, I was very ashamed of it. At first, I kept feeling that I should haul it down if there was shipping about in case anyone should see it. This would defeat the object of the exercise. That biscuit tin clanged about at the top of the mast like the bells some Eastern temples use to ward off evil spirits. Perhaps it did.

Being only about thirty miles south of the Lizard, we were plagued by birds which came flying over from their winter holidays abroad, and thought that in *Erik the Red* they had discovered their own little bit of England. They would sit on the deck, on the sails, or on the cabin top, wherever they could look most pathetic and miserable, and stare at nothing. There was never anything I could do for these creatures. They refused all food and water. Sometimes they flew off. One or two just sat and died, completely exhausted.

It was as calm and breathless as I had ever seen the sea. There was no swell, the sea being a clear blue from the reflection of the sky. When nothing moves, not even the sea, then one feels most alone.

During the night it was foggy and I could hear the thump of unseen ships passing close in the murk. Then another day of calm. But by the evening a south-easterly had got up and I was on my way again.

I was heading on a S.W. magnetic course. The idea of this was to put me well out into the Atlantic, far further west than the direct course to Finisterre in Spain. There were two reasons for this. The first was that since the winds in the

English Channel and the Bay of Biscay tend to blow mostly from the west, it was obviously good sense to edge out to the west so that we should have room to spare when going south. The westing to be made, up to the position one hundred miles off Finisterre that I was heading for, amounted to two hundred and fifty miles. This is a considerable distance to make up against the prevailing winds.

Secondly, I was anxious about shipping. This was why I wanted to keep as far off a direct line between Ushant and Finisterre as I reasonably could. Once out of the shipping lanes, the chances of being hit by a ship were almost nil.

Over the next day the wind gradually came round to the north-east, exactly behind me. It was now that the defects of my self-steering system became apparent. Perhaps it would have been all right if I had been content to consider the mizen as a steering gear only, but the sail could spread one hundred and fifty square feet of area, which was a large proportion of the total. Any attempt to get this sail to do some work with the wind aft interfered with the steering.

The trouble was that the wind would not stay at the same strength, while the shock-cord gave a constant pull all the time. So whenever the wind dropped a little, the shock-cord would have more power than the sail, the boat would gradually sweep round, and then the mainsail would gybe. Another cause was the fact that my blocks were of the cheap and primitive ironmongers' kind, not proper marine blocks. So it took a fair strength of wind to overcome the friction of these.

To make matters worse, it was now raining. Life when it is cold and wet is miserable in a small boat. There is not the room to be continually taking oilskins on and off. To go without oilskins means that one's wet clothes will take ages to dry. If one tries to live below in oilskins, the cabin mattresses and bedding become soaking wet. So with the boat not steering himself properly, I spent my time leaping in and out of the cabin to correct him.

As the wind grew stronger, I had to lower some of the main. The wind was a steady force five, which was uncomfortable for a small boat. Being so light, every time a wave reared astern, the boat would leap up instantly. When I came up into the cockpit to adjust the helm I had to hang on tightly. I now found out the disadvantage of the large and relatively high floor of the cockpit. It made moving about in it very difficult, not to say dangerous, with the sharp motion.

The boat was still not steering himself perfectly. Every so often while lying in my bunk, I could tell by the feel of the boat that he had swung round by the lee and was in imminent danger of gybing. I would leap up and rush out into the cockpit and try to correct the helm before this happened. Eventually the inevitable happened while I was sleeping. I woke up to find the boat pressed down and heading the wrong way. We had gybed! Fortunately there was no damage done. It was a credit only to the Chinese rig, but this sort of thing was ruinous on the edges of the sails where the sheetlets fouled up with the bamboos. But at least we had the wind with us and were going as fast as we could in the right direction.

Three hours later the wind had dropped and we were drifting helplessly.

These on and off conditions went on for several days. Because the sky was overcast, and due to my lack of experience with sextant navigation, exact position finding was difficult. When out at sea in a small yacht and obviously hundreds of miles from land, it is quite unnecessary to know where you are at any particular time until the boat starts to approach the shore. In a well equipped yacht, though, it can be done. With a patent log for measuring how far you have gone, and with accurate steering, you can plot the course you have been doing, and even after several days without a definite fix, arrive at a surprisingly accurate position.

In my case, I had none of these things. I just had to guess how fast we might be going by looking over the side at the water, and then guess how long we had been doing this speed. At first, too, I was always uncertain how far off course we had been sailing while I was asleep. My ancient compass had not been checked in the accepted manner by swinging the yacht round a fixed point, so this too could be wrong.

Provided that you can see the sun, taking a sight with a sextant is not too difficult. The hard thing at first is the calculation. Although for latitudes this is simple, when you first try to work out your position and come out with a figure, you can never believe it. What if my plastic sextant is wrong? Although the latitude fits in with my days run from the last latitude, what if that was wrong too? And the one before that . . . ? In fact I never found my latitudes far out — except on a later voyage.

Longitudes were different. I was using a rather primitive method, to save having the bulky tables used in the modern methods. I was able to do all my calculations from *Reed's Almanack* and ended up with a figure for the longitude which could be drawn straight onto the chart. The trouble was, that I could never believe the figure I got, so I had to work it out a second time. This answer would come out differently, so I would have to check it with a third answer, and this again would be different. . . .

All chartwork and navigation, eating, and writing was done on the same table. There was no room on the other one. To prepare for this I had folded up my charts like roadmaps, rolled charts being impossible to use. I wondered how long it would be before the charts were worn into holes.

On Sunday 16th May, it was cloudy again at noon. By the aid of Consol bearings and calculating from previous fixes, I guessed my position as 46° 25' N, 9° 20' W. This made me more than halfway across the Bay of Biscay to Finisterre and well outside the shipping lanes. I should now be able to relax a bit. Soon the wind would stay in the north because we would be in the Portuguese Trades, and even if they refused to behave, once past Finisterre we would be able to put into Vigo in Spain.

Before dusk I lit my lamp and put it on the bridge deck. The wind was on the stern and the boat was pitching about a bit. Usually I tried to hang the lamp from the mizen, but it used to swing all over the place, even when tied down, if it was at all choppy. As I was feeling tired and there was no immediate hurry, I lay down in my bunk, telling myself that I was thinking of a better way of securing the lamp.

About an hour later, there was a tremendous crash. With a start I woke up to find myself lying on my bunk in the dark. There was a thunderous roar of a big engine.

Whether I am glad or ashamed to say that I mentally checked that I was wearing some sort of clothing I do not know. At any rate I leapt up and poked my head out of the hatch.

It was thick dusk. A big fishing boat of the trawler type, some sixty to eighty feet long was on the starboard side, obviously having just overtaken me. They slowed and circled back to see if we were all right. Then after a lot of muttering, as well there might be, they set off at a good speed towards Spain.

At first I thought that I had run into them while they were trawling, but their action showed that they were simply on course for Spain, and had seen my light just too late.

I looked for the damage. It was incredibly little, considering that tremendous crashing noise. There was just a dent in the corner of the transom, hardly noticeable in the dark. The mizen was flapping about in an aimless fashion.

I had been saved from serious damage by the lightness and small size of *Erik the Red* and by the flimsiness of the gear. The fishing vessel had ploughed into the mizen which was sheeted out to port in the N.W. wind. The bamboo battens had taken the impact and the hook on the cheap sheet block had snapped instantly. Since there were no shrouds as on a normal yacht, the sail had swung harmlessly forward.

The boat itself had simply bounced away in the wash from the larger vessel like a bit of driftwood. Safe I was, but I would not like to repeat the experience for the fun of it.

This business made me wonder about what I could do if a ship hit me full on at night, whether I was carrying lights or not. The answer was, not very much. At night it takes at least three times as long to do anything as when it is light and you can see what you are doing. I resolved to stay awake at night as much as I could and at once set to rigging up the lamp in a more effective manner.

The sheet block was quickly replaced and *Erik the Red* was soon on his way again as if nothing had happened. As we sped along I could not help wondering what would have happened if the ship had hit us just two feet more centrally. I certainly do not expect to have such a narrow escape again.

Now that a ship had nudged us in the stern, the wind decided to do the same. It set in from the north-east and blew at force five or six for four days. This is rugged for a small, light boat, and uncomfortable, but progress was very fast now. I kept a better look out for ships now, but for many days saw nothing at all.

Past Finisterre we went, keeping well out to avoid the shipping lanes and fishing fleets of the Spanish coast and down the back of the Portuguese trades. All the time there was too much wind to lie on my bunk in any real comfort, especially with the primitive self-steering gear I had. Any time the wind might slacken a little and bring the yacht round on a gybe. Apart from the possible damage this could cause, it was always tedious to gybe the boat back and settle it down on its course again.

All this time I did not devote as long as I wished to solving the problems of rig and self-steering. The chores of watch-keeping, keeping gear in condition, and trying to cook meals on board was all-absorbing. Everything was new to me, and all the gear was untried. I made little attempt to do much cooking on this trip. I had a vast supply of biscuits, and several cheeses which had to be eaten before they walked off the boat by themselves. What I cooked tended to come out of tins, and was then heated in a pan.

On down the coast of Portugal we sped, and after the slow start, the fast passage was marvellous. The sun became hotter and although the wind stayed strong, the skies cleared, I could now get some practice taking my noon latitude sights. When the action of taking those became familiar, I began to treat the results as true ones.

In the following winds, I found how handy the Chinese rig is when running before the wind. The winds varied from force four to the occasional force seven in gusts. By lowering the sails a little and letting them take up in the lifts, I could adjust them to the strength of the wind. Another thing too I found. The mizen was being used to balance the shock-cord on the tiller, but when the wind varied, the amount of pull by the sail varied too. I could see the compass well enough from the cockpit hatch, so when it was raining I could either pull on or slacken the mizen halyard. This made enough difference to alter the course, and could be done in a few seconds which saved me getting wet.

Soon I learnt to use this method of correcting the course all the time. I was beginning to get idle, which is a sign of efficiency.

True north winds had set in down the Portuguese coast, and it took only two days sailing parallel to it before we reached a point where I judged we could head for Cape St. Vincent. My longitude sights were so uncertain still that I was not prepared to swear to our distance from the coast. But it must have been about a hundred miles.

Therefore I put *Erik* on a south-easterly course to clear Cape St. Vincent by what I hoped was a safe amount. It certainly was. When I should have passed the light a day later, it was nowhere to be seen, and I never did see it. Navigation was obviously not my strongest suit.

Since I was having so much difficulty in knowing how far west I was, I decided to resort to the old method of latitude sailing. This was resorted to by old time navigators, not so much out of ignorance of navigation like myself, but because they could not find the time accurately enough to make longitude sights. I was now fairly convinced that given a clear sky at noon, I could find my latitude.

The Straits of Gibraltar are on a latitude of about 36°N. By nightfall on the 25th May I estimated that I was down to this latitude. I put *Erik* on an easterly course, with the wind kindly on the beam. The self-steering rubber bands were arranged to our satisfaction and I felt now that we were romping home.

Two hours later the wind had dropped.

For four days the calm lasted, with the occasional feeble winds from the wrong direction. Sometimes there was fog and then I could hear ships hooting in the distance. In spite of my biscuit tin I felt very defenceless. Still, at least no-one could see it. It was fast becoming a rusty monstrosity.

Calms are marvellous for a day. They give the crew a rest from the continuous motion. Then they become boring. This calm was no exception. I bathed. The water was warm, but wet. I fished, but never caught anything. I mended the sails, and they looked no better for it. The twine holding the battens together had stretched slightly as if they were made of elastic, which meant that the bamboos were loose on the sails instead of binding them together as they should. I resolved to go over the whole rig with wire as in the Chinese method when we got into port.

I made a little flag pole for my ensign. This was so magnificent that I was almost ashamed to have it up. The yards of the sails were made out of old wooden curtain rails which had been thrown out of my father's Dorset rectory when it was modernised, and the only things I had found no use for were the marvellous ornately turned knobs which fitted onto the ends. One of these I put on top of my ensign pole. The pole was painted the same colour as the boat, and the ensign fixed on permanently. The pole was arranged to fit into sockets on the rudder and exactly matched the rake of the stern. As all this work had to be done bobbing about at sea, I was proud of myself. For a short time I had the best ensign pole since the days of the galleons. Even they would have been stunned.

I even made two large cleats out of a chunk of oak carved with my axe and bolted on. I was obviously getting efficient at this sailing business.

So when night fell on the 29th May at a position I estimated at about a hundred miles west of the Straits, I had a shock. On the starboard bow a light came into view, mysteriously flashing twice every fifteen seconds. Admittedly, it had been cloudy for days and I had neglected to take any longitude sights, but I could not have moved a hundred miles without a breath of wind. But the light was nowhere on the limited charts I carried. I was forced to the conclusion that it was on the coast of Morocco, and that I had been carried by a current towards it. One tends to ignore currents when sailing with them. It is only in calms that they come into their own. . . .

I understood now a strange turbulence in the water that I had noticed earlier. It must have been a shoal. All that night was calm. I was on the hop, trying to keep awake in case the wind changed and blew me into land.

With morning came a clear view of the land, only about five miles away, though this was difficult to judge, the land being so flat. Eventually a boatload of Arabs came past, and waved and shouted in a friendly manner. They did things in a more up-to-date way than I did, having an outboard motor which I envied them at that moment. But at least I knew where I was on the chart, only a few miles down the Moroccan coast from Cape Espartel, the headland which marks the southern approach to the Straits of Gibraltar. Oh for some wind!

As if by magic an easterly got up, a good beam wind for reaching up to Cape Espartel. But it grew stronger and stronger. By noon it was a good force six. We were now too far from the coast to get much shelter and the waves were steep. It was as much as we could do to steer across it. As we moved across the mouth of the Straits, the wind grew stronger still. A great black line of cloud stretched out of the Straits like smoke from a funnel. I wondered how ships managed when actually in the Straits where the wind is pressed between the mountains. It seemed incredible that anything could make against that wind.

By midday the next day the wind I estimated to be a steady force eight. At times it must have reached nine. To carry sail was impossible without risking damage to the cloth. It was also unnecessary. *Erik* lay beam on to the seas making no fuss. I just had to ride it out and watch the white sun-bright crests pass hypnotically by, occasionally spraying us with sparkling foam. For now the clouds had cleared away and the sun made the sea look blue and friendly. And it was warm!

The easterly wind lasted for two more days, gradually slackening. As soon as I could, I set course for the north. When the gale finished I made out my position to be some forty miles in towards Spain. At least when I met the coast of Spain I should know my position without a doubt — if I could identify it from the Pilot book, having no large scale chart of those parts. Also I hoped by keeping into the coast to benefit from the effect of the land on the wind, whereby the breeze tends to blow onto the shore by day, and off shore at night.

By midday on the 2nd June I was in shallow water with land in sight. I identified it as Huelva, and set off on the long haul along the coast past Cadiz, avoiding tunny nets, round Cape Trafalgar with its tide race, and into the Straits. The winds were fitful and this took two whole days. But by now the light west wind had set in through the Straits to replace the Levanter. According to the Pilot, a favourable current runs in the centre of the Straits, so here I kept.

This was a marvellous passage. Great mountains reared up from Africa and Spain till it seemed that there was no room between them and we were heading for dry land. Big ships passed by looking like toys, so dwarfed were they by the huge mountains falling into the sea.

After so much effort to get into the Straits, it seemed incredible that we were coming through at last and at such a good speed on the back of a two knot current. We flew past the Spanish port of Tarifa at the narrowest part of the Straits and soon the hump of Gibraltar was visible.

The wind was dropping as we swept through the harbour entrance and made our way to the Destroyer Pens where small yachts may lie free for a fortnight. I had been here before, so I knew the way. We moored astern of *Ariels* a 110-foot schooner, the biggest yacht I had seen. The tanned skipper served me with drinks on the after deck and gave me genuine fish and chips from Gibraltar. It was all very exotic. And after three weeks alone at sea it was very welcome.

8. Gibraltar

It was a good thing that I had brought up next to such a large vessel as *Ariels*. She made *Erik the Red* seem very small, which somehow put a better light on my performance, for twenty-four days is not the fastest passage to Gibraltar. But over a week of the voyage had been calm and for two days I had been held up by gales or near gale force Levanter. So for a single-handed voyage without a proper self-steering system it was not too bad. But in this matter, as with navigation, it was obvious I should have to buck my ideas up.

Ariels left for Cannes, but I met her again later on. This, I discovered, was one of the charming things about long distance sailing – the people in other boats you meet upon the way. I feel guilty that I can mention only a few, but too many names without the faces would be confusing.

After all, this life was not always concerned just with sailing and boats. Other things happened. Some of these were too small to mention, others so important or personal that I shall keep them to myself. To know the life in full, you must live the life yourself.

Ariels' place was taken by an Iroquois Catamaran which had come round from England too, but in many ways their voyage was far more remarkable than mine. George, the skipper, said he had been a professional yacht skipper at one time, but his crew had had no sailing experience at all. They had chartered this boat in England and sailed it round Gibraltar and had had many adventures on the way.

Catamarans are tricky craft to sail. However large they are, they can in theory be turned upside down. The crew of

Fia-fia sailed her with vast amounts of sails in strong winds. They enjoyed racing tankers and this boat could outsail them since they drove it hard like a motor-boat. This as it turned out, was the best way to sail her, since catamarans must not be sailed like a single-hulled yacht.

George was very impressed with the fact that they had done so well, and soon everybody he met began to have the same enthusiasm. He became a favourite figure in one of the main bars where he comforted his friends by telling them of his escapades. Many were the drinks which flowed his way from admiring listeners!

I was very fond of George. He was good value for money. He was an excellent salesman — of himself. But, alas, we had to lose him. The catamaran broke its tiller bar when a wind got up and drove it against the quayside. Until this was repaired the *Fia-fia* could not be sailed back to England or indeed anywhere. During the excitement George flew off to Spain. Eventually the owner had to come to Gibraltar to get his boat back to England.

The story of *Fia-fia* was a continuous background to my stay in Gibraltar. I got to know the two other members of the crew quite well, and fresh developments kept cropping up, but few of these could be mentioned here.

Incredibly, I saw George again, quite by chance. We met in a street where neither of us expected to see the other. He said that after leaving Gibraltar he had managed to get a job in Spain, and this without knowing a word of Spanish. From what I know of him I can believe it. The most unlikely people kept turning up who had believed every word that George had told them. He was a master of language.

But George was changed. He was rather bitter. One of his associates had gone to Spain with him and then gone off with all his luggage and money.

'It just shows,' said George. 'You can't trust anyone.'

When my two weeks of free parking was up, I got a tow round to the part between the harbour and the runway, the only anchorage in Gibraltar which was sheltered and yet free. It was not the ideal secluded anchorage of the travel brochures since it was only a few yards from the runway. If one could stand the noise, however, the sight of planes landing and taking off from one of the trickier runways of the world was always interesting. At this time of trouble between Spain and Britain over Gibraltar, with the frontier cut off, the planes had to turn sharply to avoid infringing Spanish air space.

There were often interesting looking yachts and sailing ships coming into Gibraltar, but one of the most unusual was a Viking ship on the beach not far from where we were anchored. One day I went over to look at it. The present owner was there and so I asked him where it had come from.

'It was made for filming,' he told me. 'It was built in Norway for £6,000, complete with engine, sails, oars, everything needed for the film. Then they filmed it from every angle for three weeks. Every picture you see of a Viking ship is this one, and they made enough film to last for any picture up to the year 2000. So you won't see another of these.'

I thought at first that he was trying to sell it to me so I changed the subject and got him to tell me how it came to be in Gibraltar.

'A number of families got together and sailed it from England. It's an open boat, but it's sixty foot long and very seaworthy so they didn't have any trouble. Here it was bought by a syndicate of three blokes. They had in mind a certain business enterprise which was going to make them lots of money. But they were unlucky and it didn't come off.

'The first one sold the engine and went off to England. The second one sold all the gear and went off too. The last was the skipper, and he had only the bare boat as you see here. He didn't have much time to look for a buyer so he sold the boat for a watch.'

He looked fondly at the boat. But it was now a wreck. It had never had even a lick of paint on its bottom. The teredo worm had got in. Every two days the boat had to be pumped out and then one could see the water spurting through the holes in the bottom of the boat as if through a sieve.

While I was there, the owner spent his spare time putting tingles, or patches, all over the bottom, to try and make the boat seaworthy. His dream was to take it somehow to Spain where he could get it repaired fairly cheaply. The death of a beautiful ship, like that of a person, is always hard to accept.

Smuggling used to be a major industry in Gibraltar. There are still those who attempt it. Marijuana is available in Gibraltar as anywhere else, but the social set-up makes it dangerous for a non-native to have anything to do with it. Gibraltar is a small place, but must still have a full-size political set up. This means that most people are related to a politician. In addition, successive governments promising more jobs in their electioneering have found that the only way to fulfil their promises has been to increase the size of the police force. This means that most people are related to a policeman.

Under those circumstances, when a scapegoat is needed, there is a temptation to pick on a non-Gibraltarian. In spite of this many young people come to Gibraltar attracted by life in the sun and cheap alcohol. They work in jobs formerly done by Spaniards, before the border was closed.

There is hope too for the most unattractive English girls. Gibraltarian girls have a pious regard for their commercial value in marriage, a situation which makes Gibraltarian men anxious to do anything for an English girl, even to the point of parting with their money. But the races do not mix much if they can help it.

The influx of hopeful job-seekers made casual work very difficult to find that year. I did one job of varnishing a mast but that was hardly likely to keep me going for long. Working on yachts in the marina was not encouraged, since the marina people preferred to do this work themselves and charge their own prices. But it was very difficult for them to stop trespassing workers.

A good friend was Harry, the pier master of the marina. He was a fine example of wasted talent. In England no-one seemed to recognise his undoubted qualities, so he had sailed down to Gibraltar in a small boat with his girl-friend. They anchored off the runway, not being able to afford the Marina charges. The Marina promptly refused them permission to land on Marina property, and Harry often told me of his battles with them and of the tricks he used to get round them.

Later they offered him a job as pier-master, which he did very efficiently, making a more pleasant stay for yacht-people who had sworn never to set foot in the Marina again. He persuaded his boss that those who wanted to anchor would do so, and that if they made life more pleasant for them, they would come and spend money in the Marina shop. This was so obvious that it was surprising no-one had thought of it before.

Originally, Harry had found *Erik the Red* a place in the Marina. When the foreman saw the boat, its paint-work peeling and a rubbing strake needing repair, he hissed:

'Get that heap out of here. The boss'll go mad if he sees it. We're trying to attract boats which have money to spend, not that sort of thing.'

Harry was furious. He went to his boss and said:

'This chap has just sailed here all the way from England. Have you seen the boat? He hasn't even got an engine. You should be proud to have it here.'

The boss agreed, but by the time Harry came back to tell me I had moved out to the anchorage. I did not see why I should feel obliged to the Marina for paying for a berth. It was as well I did this, because as it turned out I wouldn't have afforded to stay at the Marina for any length of time. Besides, it was better out at anchor.

One day a Frenchman sailed into Gibraltar. He was sailing his boat to Marseilles, but the two French lads he had on board to help him got fed up and left. He came round to the Marina and asked Harry if he knew someone who could help him sail the boat to France.

Harry brought him over to *Erik the Red* together with another Frenchman to act as an interpreter. This man was quite fluent in nautical English. He must have been. While I was in Gibraltar, he had brought a small schooner round to

Gibraltar and had had new sails made. He then offered the boat for sale.

He eventually sold the boat to an American for a good price because it was very well equipped below. The day came for the Frenchman to move off. He had sold everything on the boat except for some things he would take away in a box. The new owner was staggered when he appeared with the box. It was a huge crate. It was an enormous crate. It took an incredible amount of stuff to fill it. When the Frenchman left, the boat was rather lighter out of the water, and the new owner's face rather longer. *Ca va!* I expect the Frenchman found another boat to put it in.

Now he was interpreting for me very well and I arranged to help his companion to take his boat round to Marseilles — for a consideration, of course. At eight o'clock the next morning I was to go on board.

The yacht was a modern fibreglass English design of about thirty feet, one of the Centurion class, I discovered. She looked all right. I had my doubts about the French owner though. He was a small and ineffective-looking man and his English was not much better than my French. But he had employed me I gathered, because he was worried about the Mistral which blows in the part of France where we were going.

For two days we motored. There was no wind, not a breath. The diesel auxiliary chugged steadily on as we moved at four knots over the flat water. We stopped only for refuelling, putting in at Motril and Carthagena. Both were bad harbours to stay at.

Motril for some curious reason had quays built in such a way that it was unsafe for a small boat to approach them. Where it was possible to come alongside, there was a ledge running along just beneath the water as if to sink any boat which dared to come too close.

Carthagena was also extremely difficult. There was an inshore wind which got up in the harbour. We nearly crashed the boat into the quay. As soon as we sailed out again, the wind dropped. After another long leap to Ibiza, we arrived at

Palma in Majorca to pick up the skipper's brother and his nephew.

All this time, I was doing the navigation and this was good for boosting my confidence for the trip to come. When navigating my own craft, I always felt that I was not doing it properly. I could never be sure whether any errors were due to my navigation or to the boat going off course as is inevitable when one is singlehanded. Also with a rather inferior boat, it is hard to know how much to allow for leeway and current. At least I found that we were always landing up where we intended to go to. It was cheering.

The skipper's nephew was a pilot in the French Air Force so he took over the navigation. Half an hour out of Palma, he collapsed with sun-stroke. We revived him and after a rest he seemed none the worse, and was ready to take over the navigation again.

When there was wind, the weather was perfect for sailing. We put into little ports in Minorca, which were secluded and beautiful. It is impossible that they can stay like that.

There were two things that impressed me about my companions' outlook to sailing, things I later came to regard as exclusively French. In the first place, they took sailing seriously. They did not try to race the boat all the time, but things had to be done in a sporting manner. Although the boat had a good engine and it would have been easier to drop the sails and motor into a harbour or river, we always tried to sail in. Most other yachts in Minorca were also French, and they too had the same attitude. Some would come in under sail and get into a mess since no warps were ready to throw, and then the engines would be started. But it was considered bad style to motor in to start with.

Secondly, I noticed that when the two brothers were planning their destination, they chose a port, not for its historical interest or safe anchorage, but because of their guide book's rating of the main restaurant. Since none of us could cook much, and they stocked up with very little that could be cooked, this was very sensible. As part of the crew, I approved of it thoroughly.

The time came to sail off to Marseilles. The two hundred mile trip was expected to take two days, always supposing that the Mistral did not get up. This was what I had been taken on for. Anxiously, we watched the skies, but no northerly mistral appeared. There were calms and following winds all the way. I hope they did not feel cheated.

At Marseilles, the skipper went off to make arrangements for my return. He came back with a long face.

'There are no planes to Gibraltar for two weeks,' he told me. 'I am very sorry. But I have looked up for you the timetables of the trains. It will be best if you go to Spain, and then you must find your way to Gibraltar. Here, I have the money for the first-class fare to Madrid, and then on from there.'

I was somewhat annoyed.

'It's difficult to get from Spain to Gibraltar,' I told him.

'I know,' he said, 'but it cannot be helped. Here is the money for food in the train, and here is the money that we agreed.'

I wondered why the train from Marseilles was of such an ancient type. I was soon to find out. Spanish trains by European standards are awful. But they are fairly cheap and they are so bad that they can be fun. The train to Madrid was slow, being an Express (for which I was charged extra), but the one from Madrid to Algeciras was even slower. It was known as a *rapido* and crawled along.

'First class' in Spanish trains means that you get a seat, second class that you do not unless you are lucky. The train was full of tourists, and hitch-hikers on the way to Tangiers and it was packed. Most of those young travellers were English or American. We simply camped on the floor of the corridors, played cards or slept, shared what food or drink we had with each other, and were trodden on by anyone who came by. For a time it was amusing.

At Algeciras there was a hitch. The Spanish would not allow anyone to cross from Algeciras to Gibraltar, and so to get there one had to go by ferry across to Tangier and then back to Gibraltar, which is just across the bay from Algeciras. The Moroccan Police however were having a purge of 'hippies'. Anyone with a beard, long hair or a rucksack was considered one of those. Several of us fitted into this category.

'Go to Ceuta,' the police said, brusquely, and put cancellation stamps on our passports. They refused to discuss it.

Ceuta is a Spanish Gibraltar in Morocco. Perhaps here there was a clearing house for doubtful customers. Three of us had got to know each other, and we discussed the situation. The other two looked fairly respectable, certainly compared with me. It was plain that if they wanted to, the Moroccan police would refuse entry for no apparent reason.

At this point I began to think that the only way to join *Erik the Red* in Gibraltar would be to fly back to England and then get a plane to Gibraltar — if there was room. The situation was ridiculous.

We were disengaged from the ferry and left standing on the quay looking disconsolate. To get to Tangier through the border you could either go by bus or get a taxi. One taxi-driver surveyed us now.

'You get a taxi,' he said, 'and I get you through the border.'

'How much?' we said at once.

'Five pounds.'

This was an enormous price for the few miles to Tangier, but we looked at him, and compared to the other taxi drivers hovering about, he looked intelligent, efficient and trustworthy. Also, none of us was completely broke. We decided to go.

First he drove us to the nearest tap, held our heads under it, produced a comb, and proceeded to comb our hair till it met his satisfaction. Our rucksacks were hidden away in the boot.

As we drove to the frontier, he produced forms for us to fill in for the police.

'It is quicker,' he said. 'Then they do not have time to look at you.'

At first we thought that all this was hocus-pocus until we saw several disconsolate youths walking back to Ceuta. Other hopefuls were giving each other hair-cuts by the roadside, to convince the police that they were not hippies.

At the customs post a ragged rogue came up to the car, and spoke to the taxi-driver.

'Give him a few pesetas and he will get your passport stamped,' the taxi-driver said. We did.

A few moments later the man came back. He grinned and spoke.

'He says that the police do not like the pictures,' said the taxi-driver keeping a perfectly straight face.

He let us off with a few more pesetas and we were through the customs, sitting up and looking as dignified as we could. We hardly saw a policeman. But we passed other cars which were having a thorough going-over.

A bit later, the taxi-driver stopped at a house. He went in for a few moments and then came back. He produced 'kif' cigarettes.

'It is not allowed to bring "kif" through the border,' he explained. We asked him about the bribery. 'They all smoke "kif" ', he said simply.

Taken for a ride we may have been, but this episode had been unusual, and amusing. Later I discovered that it paid to try and swindle the Moroccans in return. Win or lose, the whole business was treated as a joke by most of them. It seems a very civilized attitude to money in a country where many are desperately poor.

One of us had come to Tangier to visit his aunt who lived there. She kindly put us all up for the night. The house was interesting. We were told that it had once housed a harem, a fact which was obvious from its design.

So I was able to return to Gibraltar again. As the ferry came into the harbour I looked anxiously to see if *Erik the Red* was still there. Although friends had been looking after him, I was always anxious about leaving him alone at any time. In Gibraltar the wind can sometimes whip the anchorage into a seething fury.

He was still there, riding placidly to his anchor.

It was good to be back again.

9. Spanish Interlude

Soon after I had arrived back, there was a nuisance which annoyed everyone. It was oil: A storage tank had leaked and there was oil everywhere. The company which owned the tank denied any responsibility for what had happened.

It covered the yachts and started to eat into the paint. Coming ashore in a dinghy was a nightmare. I had brought with me from England a very small rubber dinghy, of the sort to be used by an air-man who had crashed into the sea. It was just about big enough for me to sit in and paddle with my hands, and caused endless amusement. Wits used to call out, 'Why don't you just walk on the water?'

This was now completely unusable. Eventually too, it rotted from the raw oil, as rubber dinghies tend to, and had to be thrown away. Fortunately a friend who was working in Gibraltar and whose boat was moored next to mine, let me have an old 6 ft. dinghy in exchange for a few rope lines. This had come with his boat. It was flat-bottomed and flat-sided, was made of plywood, and was completely unsafe. Some people said it was originally used for mixing cement. But it was the only small boat that I could find straight away that would fit on the cabin top. I rigged up an arrangement so that I could skull it from the stern with a paddle, an art I learnt as a boy. This dinghy looked terrible but it worked. In smooth water it could take three people if nobody breathed.

This was the dinghy problem solved, although getting ashore was still a revoltingly messy business. The next thing was to get the boat re-painted.

Everyone had complained about the oil, but since the

company accepted no liability, most were discouraged from putting in claims for damage to their boats. We thought, however, that if we persisted, sooner or later the company would pay out some money. This indeed happened. But since it was later rather than sooner, there was still the problem of painting the bottom of the boat.

Antifouling the bottom of boats is very important. The slightest growth of weed or barnacles can reduce the speed of a ship enormously. The growth on the bottom of ships costs shipping companies millions of pounds in loss of fuel and added time to voyages. In the case of wooden vessels there is another danger, one I had seen in the Viking ship.

Teredo worms start off very small. They float freely in warm waters looking for wooden structures to feed on. When they have attached themselves to the hull and bored into the wood through a very small hole, they eat along the grain, growing larger as they do so. Several of these creatures, if given long enough, can demolish the inside of a plank.

Unless the boat is sheathed with copper or glass fibre, the only defence is paint. Antifouling paint contains poisons which further discourage the teredo and also help to prevent the growth of weed on the bottom of the boat.

The problem was one of where to do the painting. To slip the boat at Gibraltar would be enormously expensive as the story of a friend's boat shows.

Dan was an American who had bought in England a boat which was smaller than mine. His idea was to sail it across the Atlantic. That winter he came through the canals of France to avoid the Bay of Biscay and set off to Gibraltar, for some of the time with the help of his brother. He arrived in Gibraltar, but by this time he had second thoughts about the boat. It was too small, he said. So he put it up for sale.

Now Harry of the Marina had also sold his boat earlier. It was a small boat and one of the local scoffers told him he would never sell it. Harry did. The scoffer was incredulous. 'What did you sell it for then?' he said, 'Ten pounds?'

Harry kept a straight face. 'One thousand, six hundred pounds,' he told him.

The man went away defeated, and this incredible price circulated the boat world of Gibraltar. All boat prices immediately went up sky high.

A fellow American approached Dan to buy his boat, for which he was asking two thousand pounds.

'Say, isn't that a bit expensive?' protested the buyer. Dan pointed to Harry's old boat lying at anchor. 'See that little boat there. Sixteen hundred pounds, that cost. Boats are expensive here.'

The buyer went off to check this story. Everyone confirmed that it was true and Dan sold his boat for not much less than he had asked. He owed Harry more than he knew.

This same buyer had had the boat hauled upon on the slipway so that he could inspect the boat's bottom and stern. When he decided to buy the boat, he told the yard to put on a coat of topside enamel and anti-fouling paint while they were about it. This he did, and he was amazed to receive a bill for one hundred and three pounds. This time the price was genuine.

It was obvious I would not be able to have the boat hauled out at Gibraltar. The alternative was to get hauled out in Spain. This was far cheaper, but there were difficulties about this, and a waiting list.

The usual course in England when painting the bottom of a boat cheaply is to let the boat dry out between tides. In Gibraltar, however, the tide was only three feet, and it was difficult to find a good sheltered beach, even if this rise and fall had been enough.

There was a friend of mine in Gibraltar named Pete. Pete was the master ice-cream salesman there. He worked hard and led a very strenuous social life, so he had a hankering to get away from things for a week or so. He had told me before that sailing was something he would like to try. We arranged to go on a working trip to Spain.

The plan was to take the boat somewhere where there was enough tide to uncover the bottom. Here we could paint the boat for nothing but the cost of the paint and the cost of keeping alive. Neither of us had much money, myself due to low earning, Pete to high spending.

From the charts and tide tables which we borrowed it was obvious that we should have to go out of the Mediterranean to the Atlantic coast of Spain. The further from the Straits, the bigger the tides.

On the day appointed, Pete approached on the quay and was ferried across to the boat. Then it was time to get the anchor up.

Erik was moored in two ways in case of strong winds. There was the main anchor, but as the holding ground in the anchorage was not good, the anchor alone was not enough. Along the bottom of the anchorage ran great chains once used for mooring destroyers. The secret is to take a rope or chain down to one of these chains.

I had done this, but unwisely left the anchor down as well. This had somehow become entangled with a great mass of chains and wreckage on the bottom.

The water here is not deep, being only twelve feet, and it is easy to swim down to the bottom. But the water is not always warm and the bottom is so muddy that any movement ends up in a fog of mud. Time and again I dived down to wrestle with the wreckage on the bottom and loosen a few more feet of chain. Up above, Pete made coffee and plied me with cigarettes. When I had stopped shivering it was time to go down again. My lungs were soon bursting as soon as I got down to the bottom, since I was not in practice at underwater swimming. Many times I thought that we should have to abandon the anchor chain for the trip to Spain, something I did not want to do, since good anchor and chain can save one's life in an emergency.

At last the final links of chain were unsnagged, and exhausted, I climbed aboard for the last time. The sails were set, and with a good taut wind we sailed off to the Straits. I could not help thinking that after the struggle to get into the Mediterranean, it was sheer folly to leave it again and chance another hostile gale.

A good wind blew through the Straits, but it was a long

struggle. The current runs through here at two knots and because of the business with the chain, we had missed the tides which counteract the current.

It took Pete some time to get used to the feel of the boat. I decided to leave him to it and get some rest, but the wind, as is common in the Straits, kept increasing and decreasing. Sometimes the sails would gybe across with a bang. Then he would have to call me to get things straight again.

We rounded Trafalgar and headed up the coast of Spain. The water here is disturbed and mysterious, there are rocks, and overfalls which can swirl a boat about in circles. A rock which is one and three quarter miles away from Trafalgar lighthouse had only four feet over it. In a swell our three foot six inches of keel could prove too much to clear this. Shoals stretch all the way up to Conil.

Conil was where we were heading. I had discovered from my researches that this was the nearest river to Cape Trafalgar. It was said to be navigable by small craft at high water and to have a sandy bottom.

But when we arrived at the village, there was no river to be found. The beach was beautiful and there were holiday-makers speeding about in boats. None of them had ever heard of a river. Baffled, we decided to go further north to Cadiz.

Night fell and with it the wind, which now came from the north east and slowed our progress. By midnight, Pete said that he could stay awake no longer. He confessed that he had had two nights on the tiles with virtually no sleep whatever and a third was beyond him. I took over and told him to get some sleep.

The next day we made Cadiz. It is always interesting entering a new port since I never seem to have charts dealing with such things. One is liable to find shallow patches and rocks by experience.

Cadiz was a bad place to lie alongside which every boat must do there. Every so often a sudden swell comes from nowhere and leaves the boats rocking and bouncing against each other. After a few seconds it disappears and there is peace for half-an-hour until the next eruption.

We had a brief look at Cadiz. But the Yacht Club where we lay disapproved of our sailing clothes, and there was nowhere pleasant to put the boat aground for painting in Cadiz harbour. By this time, Pete had had a full night's sleep and declared himself fit for anything, so we set off for a river we had found out about called Caño de Sancti Petri.

This little river we had passed on the way up. It is entered through a series of rocky reefs. As usual, I had no chart of this place, which we reached at noon. We worked out from the tides at Cadiz that the water would start flowing into the river in the evening. I had done enough river sailing to know that it is easier when there is water in the river.

At dusk we approached the bar. There were two sets of leading marks and these were well lit with flashing lights. We discovered by nearly running onto a rock that we were supposed to change from one to the other half-way. Then we headed up what we hoped was the channel of the river.

It was now quite dark. Dimly we could see the banks of the river on either side. On the river itself were dim little lights. These we followed all the way up, when we discovered they were small boats with lanterns, their occupants fishing for their supper. There was almost no wind, just enough to steer, but we drifted up in silence on the tide, our lantern lit to show that we were not secret invaders.

After a while, we heard oars in the distance.

'I think someone's coming after us,' said Pete.

'Nonsense,' I told him, then listened again. He was right. We were being pursued up the river by a rowing boat. It hauled alongside and two policemen climbed on board. Neither of us spoke much Spanish, but enough to ask for the best place to anchor. Brusquely, they pointed out a place. We dropped anchor and tidied up the boat.

The policemen, it appeared, were not pleased to see us. The larger and more senior one picked up Pete's passport and looked at it. He nodded self-importantly to the other one and said, 'Gibraltar.'

The passport was stamped to show that he had been in Gibraltar for fourteen months. He picked up my passport and

a Gibraltar harbour notice fluttered out. I had not thought of
throwing it away.

'You come from Gibraltar,' he said, accusingly, in Spanish.

'No,' we said, 'Cadiz.'

'Your passport has not been stamped. It must be stamped
in Cadiz.'

We knew about this rule. Any yacht from Gibraltar which
is unregistered must first put in a port of entry in Spain
before landing elsewhere. Under international law, if this is
done, the Spanish cannot deny a yacht entry. In Cadiz we
had tried in vain to get our passports stamped. They were
charming about it.

'It's not necessary,' they smiled, and that was as far as we
could get.

The prospect of going back to Cadiz just to satisfy this
officious policeman was not pleasing, so we resorted to the
foreigner's infallible defence against unpleasant instructions.

'We don't understand,' we said in unison.

After some time of this, they became bored and made a
token search of the boat. They fumbled through a few rusty
tins and the senior man tried to dissect one distress flare.
Then they smiled and said everything was all right. Yes, we
could put the boat ashore and paint the bottom, but we must
ask the Captain of the Port first. Our understanding improved
remarkably at this point.

The next morning, the Captain of the Port came by and
told us we could certainly paint the boat. The best place was
over there opposite the village, which was firm sand. He was
polite and courteous, though with his white uniform and
black moustache looking like the original music-hall Spanish
official.

When we landed at the village, however, the officious
policeman was waiting for us.

'No landing,' he said. 'No stamp in your passport.'

He was called away to answer the phone, so we went into
the village anyway, bought some food, and moved over to the
other side of the river. As this was an island, though nine
miles long and joined to Cadiz by bridges, we felt like exiles.

Later, a policeman came over to see that we were up to no mischief.

It took two days to paint the boat, my crew working like a slave. Then we anchored in the river. It was now possible to go ashore and see the delights of the village of Sancti Petri. These were not much. The whole place was run for the benefit of a tunny canning factory. There were no amenities except one bar, and the people seemed a bit depressed, as well they might. Life was governed by the factory hooter.

Then having seen so little of Spain, it was time to sail back to Gibraltar. We sailed out of Sancti Petri at dawn, the unoiled blocks creaking fit to wake the dead as we hoisted our Chinese sails. Perhaps those villagers still remember the time a red junk came into their river.

Pete joined his ice-cream van, and I now had to prepare the boat for the voyage to the Canaries. Although I consoled myself that the voyage from England to Spain seemed likely to be more difficult than the one to the Caribbean, I could not help feeling that this was the crunch. Once I had set out towards the Canaries, I was committed to going all the way across if I could.

Doubts I felt about the voyage itself were not helped by such information as I could get about what I was likely to meet with on the other side. It was essential that I should find some sort of work there. I had made enough to get in stores at Gibraltar of everything I was likely to need for the crossing, but after that I faced the risk of being stranded without any means of support.

No-one seemed to actually know what life was like on the other side. Some said that the natives were unfriendly and did not like yachts visiting their islands. There were stories of unpleasantnesses and high prices of food. I met someone, however, who had worked as a crew on a charter yacht the year before, and told him about the stories I had heard.

'Don't take any notice of them,' he said. 'It's all rubbish. It's beautiful out there, and you can live cheaply if you stick to what the natives eat. I'm looking out for a job on a boat that's going there myself. Maybe I'll see you.'

10. Past Morocco

Erik the Red cannot be said to have been the most seaworthy-looking yacht to set off south for an ocean crossing. The sails were beginning to look decidedly tattered and many were the people who looked at them and shook their heads saying that they would never last to the Canaries, let alone across the Atlantic.

The masts too were looking seedy. They had been coated with linseed oil when they were first made, but this had been worn off by the rope and chopped plastic hose parrels holding the sails to the masts. It made them an interesting, scrubbed white colour. It also left the wood completely exposed to the air, and so the masts dried out in the sun. The cracks in the two masts went along the length of the masts, with the grain, a direction I was told did not matter, since it did not affect the strength. When I looked at them, I wondered. I could push my fingers into the crack in the mizen mast.

It is a fact that masts either split from getting too dry, or rot through being too damp. Of these alternatives, splitting is best if it is not too serious. Any attempt to try and stop up the crack can cause rot in the heart of the mast.

I climbed up the masts by way of the sails to inspect the halyards and lifts. They seemed to be giving no trouble. The mainsheet needed renewing. I had still not devised an efficient way of arranging this, so that it would be easy to tack the boat, yet be possible to haul the sail in tightly. But providing that we were not in narrow waters, it would do.

Drinking water was the next thing. This had to be

scrounged since it is scarce in Gibraltar, and all water has to be caught by the rain catchment areas or imported from outside. The stores were stowed away and we were ready for our first trip south of Europe — to the Canaries.

At last I felt that the enterprise was under way. After this, I thought there could be no turning back. The Canaries were nothing but islands on the way to the West Indies, and to set out for them meant that I was really committed.

So at this point I felt as nervous as I had the first time I had prepared to set out to sea. But there was one consolation.

Unless we were very unlucky, the winds and currents should now be all in our favour. The difficult part, the struggle to get into the northerly winds off Portugal, was long behind us. Now, I hoped, we could expect northerly or easterly winds all the time.

We left in the late afternoon on September 16th at 5.30 p.m. This was so as to catch the tides through the Straits. The only people who know what the tides are really doing are the Spanish fishermen. The chart has another story, and the Admiralty pilot book yet another. Still everyone agreed that this was the time to leave. I had hoped to have a fairly quick passage through the narrow Straits. They would be packed with shipping as always and even by day it pays to watch out for this. Therefore the easiest thing was to get through the Straits by night so that by next morning I should be clear of them, and able to sleep in peace.

Just before I raised the anchor, three French lads rowed across to us. These three had sailed an ancient Dragon, a small racing yacht, from France. They had no money, and their aim was to sell the boat to get back to France. In Gibraltar they seemed to live entirely on fish which they caught by swimming around the harbour with an elastic harpoon gun. Since I was one of the few people who could speak any French, I had invited them aboard and we had had tea, brewed from English teabags, and made incomprehensible conversation.

Now they presented me with their harpoon gun. I was

touched, but felt I had to refuse. They would not take it back, but rowed to their boat and returned with more things which they unloaded onto *Erik*.

Besides the harpoon gun, there were two plastic oil containers, a folding radar reflector, a huge terylene warp, a first-aid kit (rather the worse for wear), and a large pack of distress flares (all out of date and probably lethal). All this stuff they refused to have returned to them. As they were selling the boat, they said, they would not need it. Even the first-aid kit they rejected. One of them had put a harpoon through his hand and had sewn the wound with a needle and thread, but it would get better, he swore.

Colin, another benefactor, who had given me my dinghy, sped alongside in a motorboat as we left the anchorage, encouraging me. He had said he found the idea of going across the Atlantic alone quite incomprehensible. As neighbours, so to speak, we had seen quite a lot of each other, so it was sad to part.

There was a good easterly Levanter blowing, but even so it dropped off sometimes in the shadow of the Rock. Gibraltar is so high that the approaches to the harbour are sheltered from an easterly wind. On we sped across the Bay and past La Perla, a group of submerged rocks off Isla de las Palomas.

High mountains swept down to the sea and these gave the impression that the boat was crawling along with ant-like slowness, despite this favourable wind and tide.

The wind grew stronger as we approached the narrows off Tarifa. Tarifa is a rocky island holding a Spanish fort and juts out into the Straits, which are here under eight miles wide. The current runs into the Mediterranean at two knots and at this point it is compressed.

The east wind too, is squeezed between the mountains and rushes through the narrows with increased violence. Off Tarifa there are overfalls where the current has to push its way past Tarifa, and when this current meets the wind, a big sea is kicked up. As we approached the narrows the wind grew stronger still. Now we had to keep all the speed we could get.

We were goosewinged with a sail out on either side and the wind got up suddenly to near gale force. In the gathering dusk, ships could be seen making their way through the Straits. There was one not far astern. I wondered if he had seen me. It was time I lit the lamp. And we had too much sail up.

The trouble about travelling goosewinged to gain added sail area and balance is that sometimes it is necessary to shorten sail. With a light wind this is no trouble. The helm is put over and one of the sails is gybed so that both are on the same side. Then the boat can be allowed to come up into the wind. But now I was glued to the tiller. The wind was so strong that there was a good chance of doing some damage to the·sails. I could never forget too that *Erik*'s masts were unstayed.

It was plain though that I would have to do something. We were off Tarifa by this time and the boat was almost uncontrollable. Great breaking waves reared up steeply astern. I pushed the helm up. The mainsail was out to port, the wrong way if I needed to head South, so I decided to gybe this sail. It was a mistake. With a great flap, the wind caught the after edge of the sail and blew it into a classic Chinese gybe. This is a term used to describe what happens when the wind catches the sail from underneath. Instead of swinging to the other side of the boat, the sail is blown up so that it is flat up against the mast. I had always wondered why this catastrophe was called a Chinese gybe. Now I knew. The light battens were now standing on end parallel with the mast.

The wind must by now have reached gale force. In such a blow it is often difficult to know the best action to take. Turning head to wind was only partly successful. Since the sail was draped evenly round both sides of the mast, it tended to turn with the wind and stay flattened against it.

I tugged at the sheetlets, trying to loosen the battens from their iron grip. Slowly they came free. I did not like to tug too hard, in case I broke something on the flimsy rig.

With a fluttering of canvas, like a frantic bird's wings, the sail came free. Instantly, the pressure of the wind in the vastly over-canvassed sail billowed out the cloth between the battens and pushed them up the mast, well out of reach. Now all the sail was at the top of the mast, and its flapping heeled the boat over onto its side, and threatened to pull the whipping mast out with its tremendous jerks.

Foothold was difficult on the heeling deck, and the steep faces of the curling waves broke occasionally against the bows in a great shower, soaking me with spray which gleamed luminously in the darkness. I could see the lights of the ship approaching from the east, but there was nothing I could do about it for the moment.

The lifts to support the bottom of the sail were tied to a lower batten and in theory hung down in tidy loops which could be easily grasped. But the wind was so strong that these curved out to leeward in great bows, well out of reach. Pulling hard down on the sheets helped to bring the battens down a little, but not enough. After fishing with a bamboo pole, no easy task in the blast of the gale, I was able to capture one of the lifts. By hauling down the lower batten with this and lowering the halyard, the sail came down at last. What damage there was, I could not tell.

The wind has risen even further and the mizen was flogging away thunderously, but it was less trouble to deal with. But now the boat pitched and tossed in the disturbed sea, and it was plain that we were at the moment just toys pushed between wind and tide. I pulled the helm up, to bring the wind astern and got some way on the boat to avoid the ship, now very close.

The big ship passed safely on the port hand, and receded into the darkness, its stern light shining brightly. We had no sail set at all, just the masts and the furled sail to drive her along. We must have been doing over three knots, but without sail up there was nothing to steady the boat. The motion was frightful. From one side to the other *Erik* rolled with a quick motion dashing his decks under the crested tops of the waves and scooping up water which swirled over the bridge-deck. It poured over the sills into the cockpit.

On the trip to Spain. Myself with beard. Notice the mess in the cockpit. It always seemed to be like that.

Part of the mizen, showing arrangement of the parrels a batten lines. The bamboo battens were quite stiff and strong, and the sail was sandwiched between these thinner bamboos on the oth side, the two being joined I twisted wire. The parrels w made of thin rope threaded small pieces of plastic gard hose.

The tunny-fishing vessel which tried to board us on the way from the Azores to Falmouth. The long poles are used to carry the fishing lines.

Then there was a muffled banging from the starboard side. On the deck by the cockpit, a part which normally never sees green water, were rather carelessly lashed old bits of timber I had fished out of the water, and bamboos kept for mending the sails. Before I discovered it, half these had been washed away in the tremendous pressure of the water. To save the rest I kept trying to hold onto them with one hand. I could not leave the tiller for an instant.

After the ship had passed, I had gone below to light the Tilley lamp so that it would be available to bring up if danger threatened. It stayed in its home, which was at the far end of the cabin, secured by shock cord so that it would not fall over. This lamp is usually windproof.

When we turned stern on to the wind under bare poles, the wind rushed with tremendous strength into the cabin and blew this lamp out like a candle. I was now without light. But as I had to stay in the cockpit to steer, I thought I could do without it.

Once through the narrows, the wind did not increase and the breaking seas caused by the wind fighting the current flattened somewhat. Therefore I put up a bit of both main and mizen to add to our speed. For if by some chance the wind should drop, we would be carried by the current back to Gibraltar, and there we would have to wait for another strong wind. I had had enough of the narrows of Tarifa for a bit so I determined to drive him through.

The wind roared past my ears and the boat rolled ceaselessly as we rushed through the waves.

'Drive him through!' I found myself muttering like some film character. 'Drive him through!'

Ships' lights passed in the darkness but none of them came near us. We were now crossing their routes, which is safer than travelling along them. Our course was set for Cape Espartel, the north-west tip of Africa.

Soon the glow of a city appeared and a flashing light. It was Tangier and the lighthouse of Punta Malabata. There are vicious over-falls in the water round here, but we were a long way off and appeared to be on course. The wind did not seem to be dropping at all.

Soon Cape Espartel light came into view on the port bow. We swept towards it at tremendous speed, the wind still at force six. By two o'clock that night we were round the corner, with Espartel bearing east. We were safely through he Straits.

The wind was still strong. I decided to heave to and make some coffee. I had been continually on the helm for eight and a half hours to get her through the Straits. It was good to relax out of the wind.

I rigged up my self-steering system and put the boat on a W.S.W. course. The wind was rather less now, but we still kept up a steady estimated four knots. It was hard to get sleep since *Erik* was not steering himself too well. When it was light I decided to devise a better system. I had already thought hard about it, and had done some experiments. Now was the time to see if the new system would work for any length of time. By noon that day the wind had dropped to nothing. This gave me some time to rig things up.

All that day it was foggy. There was shipping about too, giving an occasional hoot. I hoisted my newly acquired radar reflector to the top of the mizen where it jangled about as the biscuit tin had done. I could not see that it could be very effective.

The plan was to keep well out from the Moroccan coast to get an offing should the wind blow from the south-west, then turn south to Casablanca, if conditions were good. I had been warned in Gibraltar that the weather off Morocco could turn very nasty. I had not learned then that the weather is always nasty on the next passage you are planning to make. Those people who have actually done the passage know better, but one always learns things from people who have found how nasty the passage is from someone else. The others are never around to say what really happens.

Generally, the winds from Morocco to the Canaries are part of the north-east trades and blow steadily from dead astern. Now, however, they refused to blow at all. By midday on the 18th the sun was out again and I had taken the opportunity to dry some teabags. These had somehow got soaked and I put them in the sun to dry out. For a while the boat smelled like a tea plantation until I realized I was doing no good. The teabags eventually found their way overboard.

Another thing which found its way overboard was my cockpit canopy. In Gibraltar, using spare bamboos, wire to tie them together, and an old canvas tarpaulin, I had built a sort of house over the cockpit. This now became a marvellous place to sit in, sheltered from sun and rain, and in a high wind the canvas could be easily removed, leaving a light, if strange-looking, bamboo skeleton. It was six feet high from the cockpit floor to the roof, and it really did look extremely odd.

There was just one snag. When sailing, every time I turned the boat and the mizen swung across, the sheets would get wrapped round the whole contraption. Then I would have to stand on the jerking after-deck, clutching the flimsy framework while I tried to disentangle the sheets. It destroyed the whole point, which was to have a shelter which could be kept up all the time, even when sailing.

There was nothing else for it. Either the sails had to go, or my poor canvas house. As I had no engine, I rather regretfully dumped the whole thing into the ocean. But I still think it was a good idea.

I also whistled. I had acquired my tin whistle with the confident expectation that by the time the voyage was over, I should be a tin whistle expert. There were several things against this which I had not thought of. It was true that I should have very little else to do but play my whistle, but when one is bored, the last thing one thinks of doing is to play a tin whistle. Also there is the question of superstition. Whistling on board in the old days was supposed to be an action which summoned the devil and produced a wind, but it was folly to turn a good breeze into a gale. Still, I reasoned that, as it was calm now, whistling should at least summon a breeze. Of course, I knew it was a silly superstition. That was why I had got the whistle in the first place, as a joke to prove the belief wrong. That was why I whistled.

Two hours later a little wind came out of the north-west.

The wind was very light when it came. It gave me a good opportunity to work out my self-steering system.

Originally I had had the mizen sheet on one side of the tiller with its pull counteracted by a few pieces of shock cord. The sail was let right off so that it was facing slightly forward. Thus if the boat turned too much one way, the sail would have the full pressure of the wind on it and this would try to pull the tiller with it. The boat then turned until there was less pressure on the sail, at which the pull was counteracted by the elastic.

This was simple, but I found the one main snag impossible to overcome. If the wind dropped, the shock cord would have too much strength, while if it rose, the shock cord would be too feeble. The boat would go off course and the mainsail gybe.

The solution was to use to balance the mizen sheet something which also varied its pressure according to the force of the wind. Quite simply that meant the mainsail, also eased off like the mizen. The two sails would work against each other and balance perfectly.

It sounded too simple to be true, but I tried it. The mainsail was swung over to the opposite side of the boat so that the boat was sailing goosewinged, and then the mainsheet tied so that it would pull the tiller the opposite way to the mizen sheet. Since the main had far more strength than the mizen, I tried moving the mainsheet further away from where the mizen sheet was tied to the tiller, so that it would have less pull.

It worked beautifully. In a wind so light that the rubber-band system would have had no hope of working, the boat travelled along steadily, dead on course. The whole force of the boat's sail area was devoted to steering the boat. If there was enough wind to move *Erik*, there was enough to steer him.

But this last point was the snag of the system, one I never overcame. It meant that it was impossible to reduce the area of one of the sails without affecting the steering. In the present conditions this hardly mattered, but in a squall it could be different altogether.

At midnight I changed course so that we were heading for Casablanca. Soon after, the wind dropped off again. It rose and fell fitfully, while unseen ships gave mournful hoots in the distance like great owls. At noon the wind was very peculiar. At one moment there was calm and then a sudden squall reaching force five blasted out of the north-east. Hastily I reefed the mainsail. The wind dropped again. Then a sudden blast from the opposite direction, south-west. This too then dropped. Again and again those contrary squalls kept coming. But they were never more than force five.

The wind settled down into the north-west, but in the night dropped calm again. We floated on a calm sea, the air warm and clear, with stars shining brighter than life overhead. It seemed strange that the Pole Star should be so low in the sky. As I went further south it would sink closer and closer to the horizon. To the south-east there was a bright yellow glow in the sky. Looking at my chart I decided it must be the glow of Rabat. I had read that it was the capital of Morocco. Perhaps I was too far east to hit Casablanca directly. My latitude that noon had been 34° 59′ N but I had neglected the considerable labour of finding our longitude by my very primitive method. If I was too far east, however, I could not understand why the shipping I had seen so much of that day should be so close into the coast of Morocco.

When the wind increased at noon the next day, our latitude was 34° 09′. In an hour or two we should be within sight of Casablanca. We sailed on and on and nothing appeared. With dusk, a light flashed in the gathering darkness ahead. What it was I did not know, not having the necessary charts or list of lights. But soon one thing was obvious. The town ahead was not big enough to be Casablanca's city centre.

Casablanca, I now realized, was that glow I had seen in the south-east. Unknown to me the current had gathered strength down this coast and was pushing us westward along the coast. I resolved always to try and get a longitude whenever I could in future, and never rely upon dead reckoning.

There was little wind, and what there was, was against us. There seemed very little point in trying to slog back to Casablanca. Foolishly, perhaps, I carried on.

At dawn as we were lying off an unidentified headland, there was a peculiar disturbance. Overhead the clouds began to whirl in circles. A blast of wind hit the boat, then squalls from all different directions. Sometimes these blasts of wind were scorching hot as if someone had opened an oven door. Then there would follow an icy gust which left me shivering. The boat sailed round in rings. Soon the whirling cloud formation passed to the north-east, leaving a south-west wind.

It was plain that this wind could not last long, but I was angry with myself for coming so far south when such a wind could have put me into Casablanca. Perhaps it was a local effect. By evening the wind had settled into the north again, sometimes north-west, sometimes north-east, changing without a moment's notice. Gradually that night it settled down to north, force four. We were foaming along. A ship overtook us on the same course, which meant that we were on the route to the south.

The next three days were perfect. The wind blew at a steady strength, though I shortened sail at night in case any squall should come. We had the current with us and the trade wind too. The sea settled down to a long, smooth, rolling swell which was beautifully restful and reassuring.

Navigation was not so successful. The latitude gave no trouble but my two methods of finding longitude gave different answers. The dead reckoning of my course gave yet another. I made a guess to average them out, and watched out anxiously on the 24th September. We could not be far from land. Sure enough a black hump appeared on the star-board bow. It was not quite where it should have been but it was near enough. It could only be Alegranza, the first outpost of the Canaries. We changed course to clear it.

The surf thundered against this great black extinct volcano, 1,000 feet high. On the eastern point, looking absurdly low against the heights beyond, stands a lighthouse. As night fell, this started to flash. Soon, as we sped along, we left Alegranza and its white surf astern. It took until the next morning before La Isletta light appeared on the bow. I had no chart of Las Palmas harbour, so when we had come abreast of La Isletta, we hove to. I lit the lamp, and got some sleep, waiting for the dawn.

11. Departure

On the morning of the 26th we came into Las Palmas. It was
not a very dignified entrance. Under the lee of La Isletta, the
wind dropped, and we were drifting in the entrance. Huge
ships ploughed past hooting at us, but there was nothing we
could do. Eventually we headed out again for a breakfast of
our everlasting porridge until the daytime breeze should get
up.

In settled weather in summer, yachts lie opposite the
entrance of the outer harbour by the Yacht Club. We were
waved to our berth by friends I had known in Gibraltar in a
catamaran called *Zotty*. I was to see a lot of them later in
different circumstances. Past the Yacht Club to the west runs
a road and Las Palmas proper. In front of the road is a
promenade and a beach. The occasional rock shows above the
water at low tide.

High above the city to the south rise the great heights of
the island, nearly always shrouded in mist, the highest being
Pico de Las Nueves at nearly six and a half thousand feet.

The Yacht Club at Las Palmas was an extraordinary affair,
like all Spanish yacht clubs. The Spanish Government's
keenness on developing sailing had led to magnificent clubs
with very few boats. This club was no exception. We were
told that it cost six hundred pounds to become a member.
Perhaps, after this huge subscription, the members could not
afford to buy boats.

The main part of the Club was a swimming pool and
restaurant. It was the top place in Las Palmas. All this meant
that overseas yachtsmen, often bearded and dressed in their
oldest clothes after sailing so far were only barely tolerated

there. Some of the club officials were worse snobs than the rich members they served, who could afford to be broader minded. One boat's crew was banned from the club. Her skipper, in spite of a certain reputation for getting on very well with Spanish men, fell foul of the officials by having a row with them.

Harry and Elizabeth of the *Zotty* were at first sight a strange couple. Harry had had a large store in London from which he had retired early. He was tall and thin, with a wrinkled, ever-smiling face, and glasses. Elizabeth was younger and, having glasses too, appeared meek and demure as a schoolgirl. Outside impressions are misleading ... I got to know both of them well.

They had made friends with one of the club members, who was a teacher. Often he took us around the town in his car to visit shops and chandlers. Once, when I had to get some methylated spirits, he insisted on paying for it. His kindness and generosity were embarrassing.

The teacher was very keen on sailing. In fact, he had not done much sailing, since it is necessary to pass an exam in Spain before going off shore, but this he was studying for hard. As a reward for all his kindness, Harry and Elizabeth asked him if he would like to go for a trip to the island of Lanzarote. We had done some repairs to their catamaran and rigged twin headsails, and those they wanted to test by a trip somewhere.

He was delighted, but could he bring some friends with him? Harry was a bit put out, for he had already asked me to 'come along to help, and four was already too many. A fifty mile trip meant that we should have to stay overnight. His friends would have to put up somewhere.

The teacher and his friends discussed the situation. Four of them were to come and two wanted to do skin diving, since Lanzarote was good for that.

'Isn't it possible to do skin-diving round Las Palmas? 'we asked them. 'Are there any good bays not far away?'

They considered the situation. Yes, they said, there was a very good bay, just here on the chart and indeed, it would be best to go there instead of Lanzarote, since Lanzarote was too far to go to. We arranged to meet them on the quay early in the morning.

That morning, at the time agreed, nobody appeared. Then, half an hour later, the teacher arrived alone. He was very angry. He had told his friends that he was making a voyage to Lanzarote, and now we had let him down in front of everyone.

He returned a book which Harry and Elizabeth had given him and said he wanted nothing more to do with them. And that was the last he had to do with us. Travel is supposed to foster better understanding between people, so we are told. It was such a pathetically small incident.

You must watch the weather at Las Palmas. Once I came back to see *Erik* drifting towards the shore in an easterly wind. A character in a large boat which looked like a Brixham trawler saw me trying to put out a kedge anchor and warp to pull the boat away from the rocks. He came to my rescue, gave me some chain to put on my anchor warp, which he said was no use without it, and took it out from the shore with his outboard-powered dinghy. Later I found that I had forgotten to lash in the pin of the stock of my old-fashioned fisherman anchor, which is as good a way as any, short of wheels, of encouraging it to slide along the sea bed.

Later, in exchange for the chain I took over to my benefactor one of the polythene containers that the French lads had given me. I told him it leaked, which was true. I wonder if he gave it away to someone else. In addition I took some pitch in a tin which would otherwise have been thrown away.

These strange presents were entirely to his liking. He was a Swede, named Christian, and an artist. Near the main square in the tourist part of Las Palmas was an outdoor exhibition of paintings, and one of the artists on display was Christian. I had often seen those contour maps of landscapes, used by army officers to demonstrate how they took The Hill. His paintings looked much the same except that they were hung on their sides and decorated with colours such as brown.

Christian spoke good English, besides the other five he claimed. He was modest about his success as a painter.

'Muck,' he said once. 'That's what the public will buy. They'll even buy dog's muck.'

He paused and grinned. He had an Alsatian dog which lived on board his boat. 'Once I scraped up some of the muck lying on the deck of my boat, I mixed it with my paints, and made a picture with it. I put the picture in an exhibition I was having.'

'Did anyone notice?'

'It was the first picture I sold. The person's got dog's muck hanging on his wall.'

His boat was indeed a Brixham trawler though it had never seen Brixham. It had been chosen as the best design of boat to sail from Africa with salt fish, but since the days of sail were over it had been left as a virtual wreck. Christian acquired the hull and now spent most of his time getting it shipshape. A lot of the fittings had come from other wrecks or else from the bottom of the harbour.

'If you want anything,' Christian used to say, pointing to the water, 'It is down there.'

He used some old equipment he had salvaged to pump air down to him while he worked in the bottom. It was in this way that he managed to keep going financially. His girl-friend Marianne had fallen from some staging and had damaged her back. She could barely move. They could not afford the medical charges of Spain, so they were making arrangements for her to fly to Denmark.

One night I was with some friends, Ian and Brownie, in *Wanderbird of Devon*, a forty foot catamaran they had built themselves. Suddenly we heard a cry from Christian's boat. It was Marianne. Somehow she had dragged herself out of her bunk and onto the deck.

'It's Christian!' she shouted. 'Something's happened to him!' Ian and Brownie rowed across to find Christian lying unconscious on the deck. All that could be found out was that he had been diving. We had heard of the 'bends' but the water here was not much over twenty feet deep.

It turned out that contamination from the motor of the air-pump had some how found its way into his airline and this had poisoned him. We covered him over with blankets on the deck since it was warm, and took it in turns to sit over him. The next day he was quite happy to go diving again. Later he moved into the inner harbour to get an engine fitted, which, needless to say, he had been given. We saw less of him, since he had to beware of thieves in there.

The thieves of Las Palmas are notorious, although now they are a dying breed. Rubber dinghies were a popular prey just then, since these expensive toys find a good market. Most people lost something. Even I, with a dinghy not worth stealing, lost my beautiful, magnificent ensign pole and ensign. Inside the harbour basin, a Finn was detailed to look after a yacht. He kept an Alsatian on board. Thieves threw it poisoned meat and managed to steal two anchors.

Usually we tried to avoid excitement and such as we had was our own fault. Like the time we did some repairs on *Zotty*. This Oceanic fibreglass catamaran started to leak where the bridge-deck joined the hulls. There is not much tide at Las Palmas but enough to put her on the beach after charting a way through the rocks before-hand. It was late afternoon.

We worked frantically to get the repairs done and the weed on the bottom cleaned off. Then I went back to *Erik*.

'Tomorrow,' I promised, 'I'll come and help you get her off this beach.'

Little did we know it then, but the word 'tomorrow' was on the lips of the police and others who saw the boat on the beach. No-one had told us that putting a boat on the beach was strictly forbidden.

'Tomorrow,' said the police, 'We shall go and arrest this English yacht. We must tell the newspapers.'

'Tomorrow,' said the newspapers, 'We will come and report on your arresting those English people. Tomorrow we shall have a good story.'

When they came down the next morning there was no boat on the beach. Harry had been too impatient to wait for tomorrow and had moved the boat off on the night's high tide. The police were baffled.

Harry and Elizabeth knew nothing about sailing when they had bought their catamaran the winter before in England. They always said they had been looking for a caravan on floats and this was what they had. But they had prepared for every emergency extremely thoughtfully, and taken the trouble to learn navigation. They were certainly better prepared than I was, and even I was better prepared than two Scotsmen in a fishing-boat type motor-sailor which had been lying in Las Palmas for some while. They were only waiting for spares so that they could get their engine working, then they were off to Nassau in the Bahamas.

Seeing the skipper climb the ladder of the Yacht Club quay from his dinghy was to admire the strength of human will as he crept slowly up. He was well over eighty.

'Do you ever think you're a bit old for sailing?' I asked him once.

He tapped his head.

'It's not how old you are,' he said, 'It's what you know up here that matters. But I've brought a young man along with me. He's only sixty-nine.'

Later I learnt that these two had made an epic voyage. Their sails blew out. They ran out of fuel. They ran out of food. They ran out of water. Just in time they were found by an American naval vessel which gave them enough to carry on. Eventually they made Miami after more than 120 days. There are not many people who could have stood such a trip.

Most of us there were waiting for the season to be right for going across the Atlantic. We could be advised on what to expect by a character we unkindly called 'Mad George' because some of the stories he had to tell about himself gave us a prickly feeling between the shoulder-blades. He was an ex-Naval man who had been across before single-handed, though this time he had his wife with him. He had been invalided out of the British Navy as a diabetic and now spent his life showing that he was more fit for the sea than the British Navy.

'The winds blow the same way all the year,' he told us. 'That's why they were called the trades. But you want to keep out of the hurricane season. That's July to October, though you should be safe by now. When we go this time, we shan't carry any lights and we'll go to sleep at night. There aren't any ships around to hit you.'

He qualified this somewhat.

'When I went across, I met up with a barquentine. It was a beautiful sailing vessel. They invited me on board and took the boat in tow while I had dinner with them. Then I went back on board my own boat again.'

I did not expect to meet a barquentine, but I was reassured by his saying that no lights were needed. I resolved not to carry any either. I had been wondering about how much paraffin I ought to carry with me, so that was one problem solved.

Food I had enough of, I thought. I still had enough porridge to last for months — if it would keep that long. Rice was also a good stand-by, and if I could not catch enough fish for any reason, I had many tins of corned beef. But fish was to be an important article of diet. The idea of living on fish gave me that Robinson Crusoe feeling. I would eat flying fish, those obliging creatures which jump out of the sea and onto your plate.

Food is not always vital, but water is. We were going into the tropic sun and it was hard to know how much I would need to drink. I reckoned on half a gallon a day minimum for twice the length of time expected to take for the voyage, if all went well. That meant sixty days and thirty gallons. This we could carry without difficulty. But there would be no spare water for other purposes at first.

Rumour had it that the water of Las Palmas was foul and would go off within a few days. For this reason *Wanderbird of Devon* went to Gomera as her island of departure. We made a date for Christmas in Grenada, if we could manage it.

George had an answer for the water problem too. He had filled his tanks with Las Palmas water on his last trip and had no trouble. I decided to do the same.

During these preparations, a friend I knew in Gibraltar arrived in his yacht, called *Busola*. Peter was a young American with glasses and a fair beard. He had bought the yacht in England. It was not a great deal bigger than *Erik* and had anchored next door to us. We had helped each other out in various ways. Now he was in difficulties.

Peter too had been planning to sail across the Atlantic. It had long been an ambition of his. He had sailed to the island of Palma in the Canaries with two friends who now had to leave the boat.

Then Peter found that he had to return urgently to the States for domestic reasons. He decided to leave the boat in the Canaries.

He soon discovered that the only harbour reported to be safe for a yacht was Puerto de la Luz in Las Palmas, so here he came. We asked Christian's advice, since he had been here for ages.

'Don't leave a boat here,' he advised. 'Unless you don't want to see it again.'

Fortunately, I knew two English lads, Roger and Mike, who were stranded. The yacht they were crewing on was lying alongside in Santa Cruz de La Palma. In this harbour there is often a long and heavy swell known locally as the Corredera, which comes when the wind is from the north-west. Although the harbour faces south-east and one would expect it to be sheltered, the waves break against the windward side and meet exactly opposite the harbour mouth, causing a swell to run straight in.

Their large steel yacht was lying chained to the quay to prevent the lines from parting in this swell, when a big ferry came in. It had no pilot on board since he was sick that day. It charged into the yacht, and banged it hard against the quay, wrecking all the cabin furniture on that side. Under the tremendous impact, the storm chains snapped, and the yacht swung round. Since the bows were tightly chained, these could not come round as well, so they twisted like a piece of wire into the shape of a horseshoe. This wreck was now waiting for repair in the harbour at Las Palmas and the two lads were desperate to get off the boat as they had no money.

We arranged for Roger and Mike to take the *Busola* across the Atlantic. Admittedly they were somewhat short on experience, but then so were we all; besides it was a chance of saving the boat, as opposed to an almost certain dead loss. Peter was now free to fly to the States.

Later, in quite a different place, I happened to ask the young crew of a yacht if he had heard anything of the *Busola*. Many people I had asked, but none seemed to know. But he said, 'The *Busola*? Yes, of course I know what happened to the *Busola*. The two chaps on board who were supposed to be sailing her across the Atlantic for this American, began to run short of money. Mike — you know, the dark-haired one — he got a job as a crew on a yacht passing through. I don't know where he is. Roger, the fair-haired one, found a girl who knew quite a bit about sailing, and she became his crew. They moved from Las Palmas to Palma. It was Christmas then, and the Spanish were having all sorts of firework displays and so on.

'There's a strange wind at Palma. They called it the Caldereto, I think. It comes from the west, but it doesn't blow all the time. Sometimes it's calm, then it blows like hell at hurricane force.

'Well, it was this wind, so I gather, that dragged *Busola*'s anchor. She headed for the rocks. Roger and his girl-friend managed to get the kedge anchor out. But by that time the stanchions of the rail on one side had been done in by the rocks. I don't know how, but there wasn't any other damage that I know of. Anyway, they let off distress rockets, but of course with all the fireworks and things going off, no-one took the least bit of notice.

'Still, they managed to get a tow off and were tied up alongside the quay. Perhaps you know that Roger was in a boat that was nearly crushed by a ferry? Well, believe it or not, early in the morning the very same ferry came in and bashed them in just the same way.

'Naturally, Roger and his crew weren't dressed for a public appearance. In fact they weren't dressed at all. They shot up

The rig, photographed on the way from the Azores to Falmouth. A line went to the end of each batten and these were joined by an ingenious arrangement to form the sheets. The sail was controlled almost all the way to the top and had very little twist. This, and the fact that the sails could be let out beyond a right-angle, enabled them to be used to steer the boat.

the boat steered
elf. Both main and
sheets were lashed
e tiller, so that they
ced one another.
-released knots were
Under the cockpit
s the life-raft; the
nt gimballed compass
e seen, and the pile
are bamboos on the

On the trip to Spain. A view of *Erik the Red*, looking forward. The dinghy was lashed to the cabin top when on passage, making opening and closing the hatch rather difficult. Notice the mizen mast stepped through the bridge deck, and the split running up it. The rope 'turk's head' was put on to strengthen it. It may have done some good.

The cockpit canopy, made from bamboos and an old tarpaulin sheet, gave marvellous shelter from sun, wind and rain. Unfortunately, it made the mizen sail difficult to handle. Here the lowermost panel of the mizen is brailed up with the lifts.

on deck to see what had happened. It was a miracle, but there wasn't much damage. But they thought quickly and pointed at the rail damaged the night before.

'The Spanish were so flabbergasted at their appearance, as well they might be, that they just assumed that they'd done all the damage. Or perhaps it was simple good will. Anyway in no time at all a lot of carpenters came on board and mended everything free and gratis. I expect *Busola* will be crossing the Atlantic soon.'

I thanked him kindly for this story. How true it was I did not know but it seemed that Roger had things well in hand.

Zotty and *Erik the Red* were to leave the same day. Preparations were hard under way. Soon everything was ready. October 17th, 1970 we arranged as our day of departure.

This was the voyage that had been in our minds for a long time, and like anything worth doing and possibly dangerous we treated it in a non-serious fashion. I bumped into Christian the night before leaving. His tall Swedish figure loitered in a predatory fashion round his paintings near the square. We chatted as I looked round at the bustle of people, the like of which I would not be seeing again for many days. Several hung round the rows of paintings as if they expected this to be the place where they would find a bit of life. A desperate-looking English girl set eyes on Christian and came over to him.

'Can you tell me the time, please,' she said, an extraordinary question in Spain.

Christian looked down at her for a moment.

'I haven't the faintest, bloody idea, little lady.'

She went away.

'I don't think you've got the right approach,' I protested. He laughed, then said with a serious face.

'When you are going to the West Indies, watch out for the sun on the back of your neck at sunset.'

He paused with a glint in his eye.

'Because if you keep it there, you will land up in Africa! Have a good voyage.'

12. The Ocean

The island of Gran Canaria is very high. For twenty five miles to leeward the trade wind is blanketed by the mountains. Here there are calms and the sea is strangely irregular and choppy, with occasional strong squalls roaring from nowhere down the mountains. Sometimes, however, there is a contrary wind blowing the opposite way to the trade wind, a sort of eddy which whirls over the high ground, and this is known to the Spanish as the *Embate*.

When we left, the trade wind had dropped off. It was almost calm. We tacked slowly out of the harbour between the great anchored ships, mostly Japanese or Korean, the Oriental faces peering down at this foreign junk.

Outside the water was smooth. A light wind from the south-east blew. It was quite the wrong way, but it was plain it was only a local wind that could not last long. The sea here is relatively cold and when the land is heated by the sun, the air is pulled in from the cold sea. By morning we were only five miles away from the harbour of Las Palmas. But now the current was beginning to help us. It could be seen in the strange ripples and eddies on the surface of the water.

The current is caused by the trade winds blowing over the sea south of the Canaries and removing the water towards the west. To compensate for this and prevent a big hole being left in the sea, cold water from under the ocean flows into this hole. The sea however is still sloping downhill towards the coast of Africa and this causes water to flow from the north down the gradient and along the coast. On the back of the cool, south-going current, we were now being taken from Las Palmas.

All that night was calm, except for brief periods of light contrary winds. The lights of Las Palmas peered scornfully at us over the edge of the sea, while La Isletta lighthouse still winked away. But slowly we were moving southward with the stream. I did not sleep. I seldom do the first night out from land. The sight of it slipping away with none to be seen again until the end of the voyage is always too engrossing to leave.

Next morning too was calm. There was a grand view of the great mountain heights of Gran Canaria sweeping up out of the flat mirror of the sea. In the afternoon came a wind from the east. We were on our way.

As we were still near the Canaries, I had to watch out for shipping. George's system of going to sleep at nights could not be used as yet, for great streams of shipping were pouring down past the Canaries to the Cape of Good Hope. Every day for the first five days out I saw a ship of some sort. There was another on the seventh day. Then nothing at all.

Our course was W.S.W. magnetic by my ancient compass. This would not take us directly to the West Indies, but well to the south. In the summer season the trade winds blow far to the north. If you head from England you would not need to go much further south than the Azores to find favourable easterly winds to the Americas. But at other times it pays to keep well south to stay in the trades. My plan was to head W.S.W. to a position 20°N 30°W, then head for Barbados on a course of west magnetic. This course had the advantage that it was easy from the hatchway to spot whether I was going the right way or not, the main points being marked on the compass in great big letters.

To make the journey more interesting I marked off the planned course into sections of a hundred miles each, numbering them by the days when I hoped to reach each one. There were twenty seven. I had been told by the owner of a thirty foot boat that he reckoned that a hundred miles a day was a good average in the trade winds. It would be pushing it a bit with a boat only twenty-one feet on the waterline, but I determined to try and get close to this number of days if I could.

It is a strange fact that yachts have a maximum speed dependent on their waterline. How near one gets to this speed is a matter of the shape of the boat, the amount of ballast, and the area of sail it can carry safely. Singlehanded, you must always watch out for squalls of wind, and since there is no watch on deck to give a warning, you tend to carry less sail in order to be safe.

During the first days I settled down to a routine which lasted through the voyage and helped to break up the time.

At dawn I would usually be up to see if anything had happened to the rig which needed attention. The tiller lines would be checked to see that the boat was on course. If I had shortened sail at night, then I would look round to see if the weather looked settled enough to hoist full sail. Also I got up just to see the dawn.

The next thing was breakfast. I had two stoves to use. One was a primus stove. It was quick, but it had to be started with methylated spirits. When it lit at once it was marvellous and did not take long to make a whistling kettle boil, with its thin bottom. The pan I used for porridge was thick and so needed a good stove to get the water boiling.

Porridge sounds monotonous, and so it was. But you got used to monotony like everything else. I had many pounds of oats — they were very cheap, and they were nourishing. To increase the protein content I used to add a large spoonful of dried milk. While the Primus was working properly, I usually ate my porridge straight out of the pan to save washing-up. Later when it started to play up and make the pan sooty, I found it easier to use a bowl. It saved washing the outside of the pan.

I found that sailing single-handed tended to cultivate extreme laziness in things that did not matter very much. In a very small boat, everything must have at least two purposes to be worth the room it takes up on board. So one gets out of the habit of doing things for their own sake. Some people of course would carefully wash the outside of the pan each time, but my only course of action was to try and get the

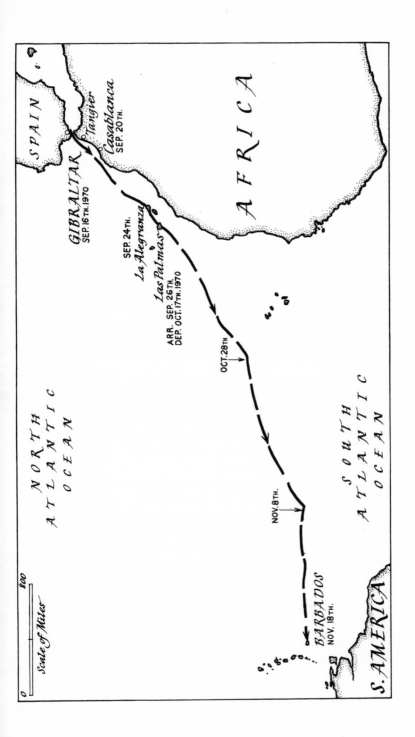

Primus working well. When I failed, the pan stayed dirty.

At first, I used to religiously use salt-water for cooking if I could. After all, it seemed absurd to pour some of my precious fresh water into a pan and then add salt to it — and salt is usually needed in the tropical sun. But there are snags about using salt-water. It has all sorts of minerals in it and these do not always have a good effect on one's inside. So salt-water is good only if you are careful not to overdo it.

After my porridge would be coffee of the instant sort, or occasionally tea. Then I could relax and smoke a cigarette.

Cigarette smoking was an absurd habit, I told myself. But instead of taking none at all and being forced to give them up at once, or taking a vast quantity which would not run out, I took a fair number, but never enough to last out the voyage. This way, I told myself, I would have to give them up. Unfortunately it had the opposite effect. Rationing cigarettes, or anything else, always has the result of making the victim look forward to the next one. The course of the strong-minded man is to throw them all overboard at once. I did not do it.

I had evolved an elaborate programme to prevent myself getting too unfit, bored, or idle. It consisted of physical exercises, and sunbathing to build up some protection against the tropical sun. I also had books I wanted to read, including Shakespeare. It also seemed a good idea to learn some Shakespeare by heart.

Physical exercises consisted basically of leg exercises and 'press-ups'. It may seem strange that in a highly physical sport like sailing it is possible not to get enough exercise. Certainly you do a fair bit of halyard-hauling and sheet-pulling. But in the trade winds under self-steering rig there is surprisingly little actual hard work to do.

In addition, a small boat is very small. Not only is there not enough room to walk about; the motion makes it quite impossible except in the calmest weather. Your legs can tend to become very weak.

I had a target of press-ups to do in a day. It started quite low and was increased steadily day by day. The advantage of press-ups is that they can be done in a horizontal position in the cockpit. This indeed was one of the merits of my huge cockpit. The floor was wide enough for me to lie across the boat. Thus I could lie down without toppling over when the boat was heeling or rolling. Any exercises involving the legs naturally had to be done in the hatchway holding onto both coamings.

This session of exercises was strenuous and extensive enough for me to find it quite hard work to finish every day. It made a good pattern around which everything else could be fitted — an ideal state of affairs.

Swimming might seem good exercise, but in fact it was very seldom possible. Strangely enough, the reason for this was my now highly efficient method of self-steering. I had several calm spells, but unless the weather was very unusual, there was always the very slightest breath of wind, even in a calm. It meant that we were always moving along slightly.

Once I looked over the side and decided that the boat was not moving at all. So I jumped overboard for a swim. The boat was moving faster than I had imagined, or else the wind suddenly increased. I saw the boat going away from me. It took some hard swimming to catch up and pull myself on board. After that, if I ever went over the side, I unlashed the self-steering system and tied the helm down.

Another snag about swimming is that it is done in salt water and leaves a thin film of salt crystals over the skin. The effect of the sun on these makes the skin uncomfortable. I found several hard, red sores appearing, which were very painful. The only way to get rid of them was to keep out of the salt water. This included shower baths with a bucket.

Every day I tried to set aside a time for sunbathing. This of course was not difficult since it was so warm and the cockpit was so comfortable to lie in. At first I was worried about overdoing it. But having been in Southern Europe for several months my skin had become well tanned and I had no trouble from sunburn.

It may seem strange, but for the navigator at sea his life is to some extent ruled by the clock. Every entry in the log is accompanied by a time and all navigation depends upon it. The problem is complicated by the fact that noon is four hours later in the West Indies than in the Canaries. The time difference must be allowed for on the way across.

In the morning about four hours before noon, it would be time to take the morning sextant sight. If, as sometimes happened, it was cloudy in the morning, then I would have to leave the sight taking till four hours after noon. This is the best time interval for taking sun-sights to get a longitude. Really such accuracy is not important. We were hundreds of miles from the nearest land, and besides, there was no way of checking the result to see if it really was accurate. But this seemingly pointless occupation had its uses. By making a great thing of navigation, I learned to avoid the otherwise inevitable lethargy which kept telling me not to bother too much about it. I had missed Casablanca for this reason. The next time I made a mistake might be altogether more serious.

Filling in the log was another case in point. This too, although only an old exercise-book, gave the voyage some sort of status.

During the morning of course I would do my exercises, read, or think about how to improve the running of the boat. Actual work on the boat was very difficult to do because of the motion. Sail-mending, which was frequent, had to be done during calms when it was safe to sit on the cabin-top — where the tools, or oneself, could easily fall into the ocean if it was rough. I worried a good deal at first about the sails chafing against the masts, the parrel lines wearing through, and the sheets fraying to pieces.

This last was the only serious chafe. The blocks I had, the cheap, ironmongery kind like all of them, were indeed cheap and easy to replace, and gave no trouble, but they were not the kindest to rope. Fortunately I had some lengths of thin nylon line. This was strong and was resistant to chafe, but as it was of the plaited kind, if it did wear through it was impossible to splice. I solved this problem simply by tying a knot in it. It looked unseamanlike, but it worked.

Otherwise I only had to oil the blocks every few days, and

the boat drove on, steering himself by magic. The rudder hangings, which used to worry me at first, were impossible to oil. I often wondered what I would do if anything went wrong with these vital pieces of gear.

The secret of easy living on a boat is to cut down the number of moving parts. This includes engines, generators, winches, and all the other noisy mechanical toys many yachts have on board. With some of them, the only non-moving things were the boats themselves, since they were always in harbour for repairs to their engines, generators, and winches. But I must not run down these valuable things. Later I was able to make my living out of them.

Soon it would be time for lunch. Lunch could be had before, during, or after the noon sun-sight. The decision was not very difficult since lunch consisted of milk made from my marvellous milk powder. This stuff, called Miracle Milk, was not available for retail sale, but I got large quantities from a cash-and-carry store to be a protein supplement if I could not manage to catch any fish. With some fruit it made a good lunch.

Of fruit I had a fair bit, including some vegetables, and a lot of Spanish onions. I had been given some when I left by an English member of the Las Palmas Yacht Club who actually went out in a boat and sailed. I shall always be grateful to him. The vegetables and onions made a valuable supplement to my evening meal.

The actual taking of the noon sight was an easy matter, unless I complicated it by practising a method of getting the longitude at noon as well as the latitude. I also spent hours working out a method for finding the longitude with a sextant without knowing the time. In theory it worked, but in practice it never did.

From my morning sight with the aid of the latitude I had just obtained, I would then take ages to calculate the longitude. It is a curious thing, but I can wrestle with figures on land and usually get the answer first time. At sea, however, concentration is more difficult. There is continuous movement, there are bangs and strange noises from above. All these were distracting. I found though that eventually I could learn to concentrate. I had to.

My only difficulties with navigation resulted from trying to do things the hard way. Any dependence upon things mechanical, electronic, or mathematical used to annoy me exceedingly, since they were not really under my control. So I was always trying to think up ways of doing without them.

At last I would get a figure giving latitude and longitude. This would be compared with the dead reckoning, or guess at my position, and put on the chart with a proud cross like those for buried treasure. This would then be compared with the hoped-for position for that day — the one I had marked in before starting the voyage. There was always a great sense of achievement from this tedious, and I suspected, useless occupation. The sight of the tiny crosses advancing towards the West Indies gave me a feeling of disbelief. Am I really here? Am I really doing this? Are we really moving, or is it my imagination?

My methods of navigation will be discussed later, when I describe the times when I actually knew what I was doing.

In the afternoon, my routine of exercises would begin again. There was always plenty to occupy me at first, when it was all new. Every time I put my head out of the cabin hatch I would look round eagerly in case there was a ship in sight, or some strange spectacle. But there was nothing. Birds, and clouds, and sea, and perhaps the occasional sea creature. But under the whole blue sky there was nothing else. At first I used to have a private joke with myself as a dig against George in Las Palmas, and as an exercise for my lungs. Whenever I poked my head out of the hatch and saw no sign of a ship, I would bellow in mock surprise at the top of my voice to no-one at all, 'What! No barquentines?'

The joke began to wear thin when I realized how many times I had said it, and each time it had been more than true, for we were in thousands of miles of nothing. But it was all beautiful.

Another activity to keep my voice in fettle consisted of reciting Shakespeare to the seabirds to improve their education. The secret of single-handed sailing, I discovered, is to turn its disadvantages into advantages. After all, where else could you rush about with no clothes on shouting at the top of your voice?

All reading was done in the afternoon, or in the evening after supper. Another activity I engaged in was producing ideas for different designs of yachts. Some day I would like to design a dream boat, but each idea is so different from the last one that I doubt if a yacht would ever get onto the drawing-board, let alone off it.

Supper was almost invariably curry. By long and bitter experience I had found that this had almost overwhelming advantages. It would disguise the taste of unpleasant tinned meat or fish, yet not disguise that of good food. It was ideally suited for having with rice, which is cheap to buy, easy to stow, and simple to cook. And it was possible to eat it almost every day without getting too tired of it.

I always seemed to be economizing on food. It was not just because of shortage of money. In a small boat there is only a limited amount of room for stowage, and to take vast quantities of food on the off-chance that the voyage might last for twice as long as expected is not always possible. So I tended not to eat too much until the voyage was well advanced.

An eating plan which I found a good idea was to save some luxury, however small, like a tin of an unusual delicacy. This was consigned for eating at a time of celebration, such as the halfway point of the voyage. Any food which I was short of, and which I considered a luxury, like tinned fruit, was rationed out by the week. It was just one more thing which gave an added shape to the voyage.

After supper and coffee, I could light the lamp for a couple of hours, listen to the radio, or read. Before it got dark, I often shortened sail for the night. Many times though, mindful of those daily marks which were slipping behind my imaginary programme, I decided to risk keeping up full sail.

In the evening after dark when the radio reception was best, I could listen to my little radio. It could only pick up the medium and long wave bands, so its range was not great. It was mainly of use for the time signals which were used to correct my rather erratic watch. Day by day the programmes, even the Spanish ones, grew fainter and fainter, and I began to worry about time signals. Soon we would really be on our own.

At night I could sleep. But I had my invaluable alarm clock. It was set to go off every two hours if the weather looked unsettled, or every four hours if things seemed set fair.

It was always a strange feeling lying in my bunk like a caterpillar in a cocoon. The boat would be rising and falling on the swell, the parrel lines creaking against the masts, with the occasional jingle of the sheet blocks as the boat yawed a little off course.

The moon if it was up, shone in through the cabin hatch, big and bright in the tropical night sky, or giving a sly, slit-eyed gleam if it was just a crescent, and casting strange shadows out in the cockpit. Always, without ceasing, a few inches from my ear, the rushing of the water as the wind pushed *Erik* through the seas. Down there, listening to it, I could imagine that we were shooting through space at thousands of miles an hour.

Sometimes I woke up to strange lurchings of the boat. It would take some seconds to realize that we had gybed. This often happened if the wind dropped off and then got up again suddenly. It was always ruinous on the sails. I would lever myself out of my bunk to go on deck and put the boat on the right gybe and adjust the steering gear. In the dark it was a tedious and time-consuming business.

Then I could go below to my bunk, and console myself into sleep with thoughts of the sail repairs I would have to do the next day. It was one of the big disadvantages of the Chinese rig.

13. The Rig

The sails I had made directly after the Chinese pattern, but adapted to the design I was using.

Erik the Red had two masts like a European ketch, the tallest being forward. These masts were completely unstayed. At first I was afraid that the extra strength would add to their weight and affect the stability of the boat. This was not so. Since there are no compression strains from any rigging, the mast can be allowed to bend naturally. It is true to say that the masts need only be light because they do not have to support a lot of rigging.

The main mast is about thirty feet above the water, while the mizen is twenty-six feet. On each mast is carried one Chinese sail. There are no staysails, spinnakers, jibs, or spare sails.

The Chinese sail is not a lateen sail or a square sail. It is in European terms a fully-battened, balanced lugsail, part of it projecting before the mast. So the sail tends to be more efficient on the tack where it lies away from the mast. To try and counteract this and to prevent the boat being completely useless on one tack, the main was hung on the starboard side, and the mizen to port. When I was actually trying to go to windward, I used to feel that this made the boat go equally badly on either tack.

The battens are fairly stout bamboos, and not intended to bend at all. They are attached to the side of the sail next to the mast and bear directly on the mast itself. On the other side of the sail are thinner bamboos. Pieces of wire are pushed through the sail cloth and go round the two battens like a sandwich. The wire is passed round twice, twisted with a pair of pliers, snipped off, and the resulting end pushed out of the way under the bamboo.

The parrels are very important. They are short lengths of line going round the mast to each bamboo. To help them slide up and down the masts, these lines were threaded with pieces of chopped plastic hose strung on like beads. This primitive system cost virtually nothing, was easy to repair and worked extraordinarily well.

The other equipment which was vital for easy working of the sail was the system of batten lines. Each one was attached to a batten abaft the middle, and led to the forward end of the batten above. It is important to get the tension on these lines exactly right. Their purpose is to stop the battens pressing forward as they are otherwise bound to. So in theory, when moving the lower batten forward or back, the whole sail moves in unison. I managed to arrange things so that only the lowermost parrel was actually pressing against the mast to stop the sail swinging forward. The batten lines kept all the other parrels away, and made hoisting and lowering the sails extremely easy.

As a result of this system, I was able to dispense with a good deal of the arrangements which the Chinese junks use for the same purpose. Having a small boat, I could get away with it, since if anything tangled up, it was not too heavy to deal with by strength of arm. But in a small boat, the less bits of string to pull and trip over, the better. There was a good deal of adjustment needed by trial and error, however, until everything worked properly.

One of the charming things about bamboos, besides their cheapness and lightness, is the fact that they have convenient bulges every few inches. Thus any lines attached to them are simply tied round and cannot slip along them. It made adjustment very easy.

Attached to the next-but-one lowest batten are the lifts. There are two on each sail, one forward and one aft. They are arranged so that the lowermost panel, which is smaller than the others, can easily be furled up out of the way. This I

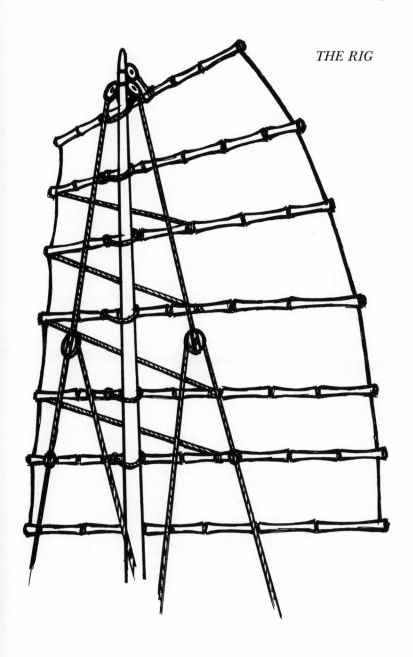

THE RIG

often did. When reefing, this panel always had to be furled up like this to start with, and also when lowering the sail.

The Chinese system of lifts is ingenious. It doubles the power of a pull on the downhaul, and so helps to take the weight of the sails when they are fully down and resting on them. Since they lead down either side of the sails, the battens neatly drop down in between them. Thus no tiers are needed to put round the sails except in the cause of neatness, which is hardly a cause at all. The sails could always be got rid of instantly, and, except in the case of extremely bad management, never got out of control, with canvas flogging dangerously and expensively in all directions. They are far too well-mannered for such excitement.

The over-whelming advantage of this system was that reefing was done simply by lowering the sail by as much as one wanted. The lower battens simply fell into the lifts and in normal conditions needed nothing more done to them. In very bad conditions, or in harbour, where only a tiny sail is needed for coming up to a mooring for instance, just the top panel or two could be set.

If the wind was strong, there was a tendency for the cloth between the battens to billow out into a curve and pull the lower battens up the mast. This I cured by using one of the spare ends of the lift lines to tie round the parrel on the batten of the lowest working panel. The lift tail-ends were both secured round the same cleat, since there was hardly ever a time when they were not both needed at once. This saved weakening the unstayed masts with another cleat. When they saw this, the yachtsmen who believed they knew what was correct always had the horrors.

Another thing which struck many as quite extraordinary was the type of 'block' I used for my lift lines — porcelain insulators designed for electric fences and so on. I had found them on a rubbish dump, and I did not want to waste them. They made the boat look like a floating wireless station, but they were effective and foolproof. They were used even at the masthead, put on strops which fitted loosely over the top of the masthead. The blocks too were strung from rope

SHEETING SYSTEM

MIZEN

HAUL IN AND TIE SLIP-KNOT
TO SHORTEN WHEN REEFING

MAINSAIL

ENDS OF
BATTENS

strops in the same way. A chock screwed a few inches down the mast stopped the strops sliding too far down under the strain.

The most complicated-looking part of the rig is undoubtedly the sheeting system. Admittedly, it is somewhat clumsy, but really it is very simple with almost nothing to go wrong. Every batten, but not the wooden yard at the head of the sail, has its own sheet. These are connected by an ingenious arrangement, using my insulators and pieces of wood with holes drilled through them. The Chinese invented this, not me.

The idea is that the whole sail is supported throughout its length, so that there is no particular strain on any one part, as with the Western yacht rig. By a system relating to the law of mechanics, so I am told, there is more pull on the higher battens, where the narrow angle would make one expect less. Thus the sail has no tendency to sag off to leeward at the top. Many of the old Western rigs had a very considerable rake aft on the masts. This was to make it harder for the gaff to swing outboard and let the sail sag away from the wind. But the Chinese sail is supported at the top.

For this reason, the masts of a Chinese-rigged boat can rake well forwards. It looks most peculiar by Western standards, as if the boat is turning into a submarine, but it does mean that if the sail is left to itself, it will swing outboards. The sheet is used to stop it. So whereas a conventionally rigged yacht needs the boom lashing out when running in light weather, this is quite unnecessary with a Chinese sail.

It is this aspect of the sails in calms which is so restful. There is no banging and crashing of the boom as the boat rolls. There is no knocking of the wind out of the sails in a swell, and the sailcloth sits up there quietly without flapping about.

Still, this sheeting system has its snags. Since the arrangement takes up so much room, the main sheet must be led to the windward side of the boat. There is no way round this. So, when tacking, the sheets of each sail must be led round the battens to the other side, the block hooked into an eyebolt, and the whole sheeted down. This, to say the least, was tedious, and in tight conditions in anything of a wind, was quite hair-raising. The sheet lines used to tangle round the battens, interfering with the set of the sail. With the original suit of sails, disentangling these was extremely difficult, and almost impossible with the sail let out.

Once I nearly went overboard trying to disentangle the mizen sheetlets. To do this, I had to stand right on the after deck and try to twitch them round. Suddenly, *Erik* gave a lurch and I lost my balance. I was left hanging between the sheets and the boat with my toes just on the deck edge. Fortunately, the feeble lines and bamboos were strong enough to take my weight.

The cloth for the sails was the stuff bed-sheets are made out of. I saw some unbleached cotton sheeting advertised for mail order, and bought a quantity. Although I made the sails myself, they lasted for some time, considering everything. They could not compare with modern terylene yacht sails, but then there was no comparison in price either.

Many people used to ask me if the Chinese rig is the easiest to handle. I always told them it was marvellous — if you had an untidy mind.

I made the lower battens all parallel to each other and horizontal. The thought behind this was that when I wanted to reef the sail, there would be no need to touch the lifts and adjust for the difference between the force and after part of the sail. Later, I wondered about this.

An operation which is often necessary when reefing is the adjustment of the sheets. It is obvious that with the sheets going to every batten, as the sail is lowered and the battens get closer together, the lines will get longer and longer, until it is impossible to sheet the sail in close-hauled. For this reason, the Chinese have as much of the sheet as possible in one continuous line. This was the system I used too. The line ended in a knot at the multiple bullseye and to shorten it, I simply hauled it in and tied a slip knot when it was the right length to prevent it from slipping out through the hole again.

The end of this line used to dangle about looking untidy but I could never think what was the best thing to do with it. Usually I just let it drag over the side in the water out of the way.

All my lines were poly-propylene which I bought cheaply by the coil, or in offcuts from the local netting factory in Bridport. When I set out, people said that this stuff would fall to pieces in the tropic sun and this worried me at first.

What about repairs? Well, these were continuous. I must confess that I got fed up with the little rips which kept appearing. I began to wonder if I would get across the Atlantic with any sails left at all. It would be disastrous to be left drifting in mid-Atlantic gradually running short of water. Later on, I began to discover ways of overcoming this problem. The main damage was done when the boat gybed. The sheets would get tangled round the battens, and instead of pulling on the ends of the bamboos as they were supposed to, would pull on the cloth in between them. This would give way under the strain and rip along to the next seam. The more the sail ripped, the more strain there was on what was left.

Another vulnerable part was the front edge of each sail. Thought about the system of batten lines will show that all the strain is transferred to this edge. If it is not strongly made, sooner or later it will rip and a tear will spread along the panel, making the sail useless.

In spite of all those disadvantages, one fact remained. The self-steering gear, using just the ordinary working rig of the boat, was a success. No wind vanes, extra sails, or auto-pilots. Nothing elaborate or expensive. I had much more confidence in my boat now that he could matter-of-factly steer himself across the Atlantic under his normal sailing rig.

It cannot be claimed that the Chinese rig is the best sailing rig. To windward in a choppy sea, it was of very little use at all. In harbour though, we could tack in against the wind like any normal sailing yacht — if the sails were not too tattered. The big asset for *Erik* when close-hauled was that he could be left with the tiller lashed and would sail happily, if slowly, on a dead straight course. For sheer convenience, I would put this quality above all as essential for a boat used for single-handed sailing. In my spare time, I put in a lot of thought about how this could be achieved with the wind aft too.

14. Towards the Land

After that calm first day, for the next five days we averaged one hundred and ten miles a day. My calculations of longitudes I was now confident about, so I could be pretty sure that my distances run each day were right, especially when stretched over a period of days.

It was a marvellous start to the voyage. Despite that disastrous first day, we were now only forty miles behind the mark for the imaginary one-hundred-mile-a-day voyage I had marked on the chart. But it was plain I could not keep this speed up in such a small boat. In theory, a boat of *Erik*'s size should have a maximum possible speed of six knots. This however, was in ideal conditions — not rough, so that rolling would slow the boat down, yet with enough wind to keep the boat pressing on all the time. Such conditions were very rare over a period of twenty-four hours. The wind used to vary between force two and force five.

In spite of my good progress, or perhaps because of it, I had decided not to rush. Every night for those first few days, I carefully lowered sail at night, usually just the main by one panel. At first I reefed the mizen by one panel as well. But this sail was so much smaller and, being by the cockpit, was so much easier to get at, that I used to lower the main alone later on. To my delight, I found that my lazy method of altering course would still work with the new method of self-steering. I could correct course just by pulling on or slackening off the mizen halyard a fraction.

The annoying thing about reefing down for the night, was that, if I did, the wind would invariably drop off very light in the middle of the night. I would wake up to feel that we were hardly moving, so I would go out into the cockpit. The breeze would be light and warm, and the boat sneaking along at about two knots. Then I would succumb to the temptation to hoist full sail and risk an increase in the wind.

If the wind did get up strongly in the night, it was often awkward to reef. Not only was the actual shortening of the sail more difficult in the dark, but so was the adjustment of the sheets to the tiller. The snag was, that if I lowered part of the main first, this would lessen its pull upon the tiller, thus bringing the boat a little into the wind. The main, still by the lee, or the wrong way into the wind, would swing round until it was pointing towards the bows, the enormous area pressing the boat on its side until the deck was half-under water. I would then have to speedily rush along the higher side-deck to either adjust the lines on the helm, or lower the mizen a little to balance the pull of the main. Then the sheet lines would have to be taken in and this was a job made more difficult and dangerous by the darkness.

After the first week the wind began to slacken off a little and here the Chinese rig on my small boat came into its own. In total area, the rig was large, with the main at 260 square feet and the mizen at 145 square feet. Normally a boat of her size would not have much more than 300, but this would be supplemented by big light sails in calm weather. These I had none of, so I was forced to rely on only two sails.

Those two large sails would hang out happily and catch anything in the way of a breeze that was going. With the weight of the battens pulling the sails out, there was no way in which they could flap and bang about. Stealthily we would ghost along. Even on the day of the lightest wind, almost a flat calm, we made forty miles with the aid of the current and those sails.

For the first eight days until the 24th October, the wind was in the north-east. After that it began to come round more southerly until by the next day it was in the south-east. The self-steering arrangement refused to work so far into the wind. It was marvellous with the wind on the stern, or on the quarter, but once the wind came round so that it was on the beam, it was impossible to get the sails so that they could truly be called goosewinged. The main would by that time be pointing almost to the bows so that it could be at a wide enough angle to the mizen. It was obviously wrong for sailing with the wind on the beam. At times when the wind would get up and hum viciously through the rope lines and tap the halyards against the masts, the main would be flattened against the wind, the sheets bar-taut under the tremendous strain. The mainsheet would be tied round the tiller right against the rudder stock in order to lessen the pull against the mizen sheet, fastened right at the very end of the tiller.

The force of the wind on the mainsail would push the bows down and press the boat through the water, the crest of the bow wave foaming onto the deck. Anxiously I would stand and watch the uneasy motion of the boat and wonder if I should reef, or head off on a more westerly course. But now we were already on a westerly course, when my aim had been to head to the south as much as possible.

I would go below, hoping for the best. Later the wind would disappear unseen into the night, and this would upset the balance of the helm. With a great flap, the main would gybe ruinously round. I would then have to go on deck to set everything to make *Erik* steer properly, and we would go even more off course.

By the small hours of the 26th, the wind was well into the south. I could no longer go anywhere near the right direction while goosewinged. So I brought the main round to the starboard side, sheeted the sails in, and lashed the helm. We were on course and somehow going at the same three knots. But those conditions only lasted for a night.

The trade winds, I found, then set into a regular pattern. The usual direction was slightly north of east, but this would vary from north-east to south-east by our compass. This change of direction was continuous. It made me realize why square-rigged ships were best for sailing with the wind. With a fore-and-aft rig, though rather less so with *Erik*'s, it was necessary to gybe as the wind came by the lee. This had to be done in plenty of time, or the sail might gybe accidentally with disastrous results. For me, this meant either letting the boat go off course slightly, or else having to gybe round. If I had not had to use the sails for self-steering, it might not have been so necessary, but as it was, the wind would come round so that the mizen blanketed the main. It made it impossible to balance one sail against the other.

I became sick and tired of gybing the sails. The main-sheet line and block had to be unlashed from the tiller, passed round the other side of the mizen mast, and hooked up again on the other side of the tiller. Often I tried to do this without coming up head to wind. It required some quick thinking. The pressure of the sheets on the tiller was surprisingly large, and if I removed one, it required all my strength to push the tiller against the other. Sometimes I failed and the boat swung into the wind, the mainsail gybing over and leaving everything in a tangle of lines. Just lashing the tiller did not work, except for a few seconds.

The easiest way to change gybes was to use shock-cord as with my old system. This steered the boat beautifully for a while, if arranged so that it replaced the mainsheet. Discovering this, I had bought a good, strong length in Las Palmas to replace my tatty old pieces. As I left the port I tried to devise a system of fastening it securely to the boat, and in doing so dropped it overboard.

On the 28th October came an important stage of the voyage. Our position at noon was 19° 31′ N, 30° 15′ W. We were now past the magic mark on the chart where we could turn directly onto a westerly magnetic course. In eleven days we had done over a thousand miles. There were less than two thousand to go. It was an exciting moment. To celebrate, I dug out one of my delicacies — pheasant breasts in aspic. It was nice for a change.

After the change of course, I began to realize the sheer size of the ocean. We had been going well. I had been keeping the boat sailing as fast as possible. Everything had been in our favour. Yet we were still little more than a third of the way.

Somehow, this was more depressing than if we had been caught for days in calms. At least then you can look forward to better. But now I could not expect to have better conditions than we had had already. And even then, we were not half-way. What if we should have really bad luck for a change? How long would it take then?

By this time however, I could be a bit freer with my water. Having done a thousand miles I need only allow twenty gallons for the rest of the journey. I had only used two so far. That meant five gallons in hand. It felt like a treasure of gold. It was now time to replenish my water tank.

The water arrangement on *Erik the Red* was one of the most primitive. There was no tank built into the boat which is the usual practice. I could not afford it. Instead, there was a polythene container of five gallons capacity, originally intended for paraffin. It was complete with a tap and lived under the bridge deck. It sat on two biscuit tins containing some of my everlasting porridge and was secured to the mast by a piece of old shock-cord to stop it from tipping over. The porridge lasted longer than the tins which eventually rusted away and collapsed. Later I used Coke boxes.

To fill up this container there were three large five gallon containers and ten small gallon ones, of the sort used to contain catering supplies of orange juice, tomato ketchup, and the like. The small ones sat under the after part of the cockpit floor and could be used as they were, which was often convenient if there were several days of rough weather.

To fill up the ready-supply container, however, was harder work. First the cockpit floorboards had to be lifted up. This in itself was not a difficult task, but unfortunately the cockpit always seemed to be full of all the things for which there was no room elsewhere and which would not get spoilt by the weather. All this junk would have to be cleared from one side so that one half of the floor could be lifted. A container, weighing over fifty pounds, would be lifted out and deposited in the cockpit, while I lowered the floorboard, trying not to catch a toe in it.

This heavy container would then have to be lifted and put

on the bridge deck, where it did its best to fall over with the motion of the boat, usually when the top had been removed. The ready-supply container complete with funnel was then placed in the cockpit, and the water was poured over my feet, some of it going into the container. When full, this had to be carried below and shunted under the bridge deck. Eventually I abandoned this wasteful and strenuous method and used a length of plastic garden hose to syphon the water into the container without removing it. I should have used this simple idea to start with.

There was now a good strong breeze from force four to five. The boat began to roar along at speed again. But I was starting to worry about my navigation. After the days of light winds, our distance run during the eleventh, twelfth, and thirteenth days worked out at three hundred and sixty miles, which meant an average of one hundred and twenty miles a day or five knots. For such a small boat, this was too good to be true. I decided I must be doing something wrong in my calculations. My watch, which I had timed to be gaining exactly forty-six seconds a day had immediately begun to be erratic as soon as we set out across the Atlantic. Yet, from Gibraltar to the Canaries, it was perfectly regular. Perhaps this was the reason.

I had now lost contact with the shore. My small and ancient transistor radio could not compete with the distance and after twelve days was unable to get even the strong Spanish programmes and time signals. As far as navigation was concerned I was on my own.

In fact it was not long before I picked up Radio Montserrat, over one thousand miles away. Its time signals, I discovered later, could be up to two minutes out, which meant a difference in longitude of twenty-five miles. But it was near enough for us. I carefully did not note picking up Radio Montserrat in the log. I always felt that this radio business was cheating, and that somehow it spoilt things to get a sound from a shore so far away, and to be tamely provided with time signals. This was silly.

During those first days another annoyance developed. The

masts, which had been well wedged in at the foot and at the partners, began to shift about. The mizen mast seemed to be suspended at the partners and in the heavy rolling which sometimes developed would swing from side to side, banging the socket of the step with a leverage force equivalent to many hundreds of pounds.

'Bang, bang' it went as we rolled, and as an accompaniment the tin plates and pans would clink and clank in sympathy. It nearly drove me mad. I managed to wedge the foot of the mast temporarily by pushing a chisel down between the mast and the biscuit tins, being too idle to remove those rusty monsters in that rolling hell. The banging stopped for a few days.

This left only the rolling. *Erik the Red* was flat-bottomed and the sides slopped inwards from the deck, so this helped to cut out rolling. But when the wind was exactly on the stern under his goosewinged rig, then there was not much to stop him. He did not roll much either way, but the motion was sharp and made it difficult to rest below. There were no bunk boards to the bunks, since I always used the downhill one, but during rolling sessions when the downhill bunk and the uphill bunk changed places every few seconds, this was no good. I found that the removable galley sideboard shelf could be propped against the cabin table, and wedged into a gap at the bottom of the bunk. This was simple, yet it worked.

Later, when I realized that a few degrees off course mattered not very much, I used to purposely set the boat slightly off course so that the wind was on the quarter. *Erik* thus heeled slightly one way, and the rolling was cut out completely as we sailed on.

On and on and on.

What a strange feeling it is to sail a small boat alone in the middle of an ocean! It is a feeling of such unreality. The boat himself seems to have purpose enough, but what of you? What are you doing here being carried endlessly over surging waves in a world of nothingness?

This is when there is a danger of hallucinations, of strange dreams, and fantasies. Many, many times you feel them pressing in upon the corners of your eyes to try and find a foothold in your mind.

Is it wrong to push them steadfastly out, to set your thoughts upon the boat, the sea, or anything real, to stop the beasts of the mind from stalking up on you? What insights, knowledge, great thoughts might fill your brain if once you left it open!

But you don't. For you are afraid of what might creep in besides, and take over that strange reasoning which keeps you holding the boat upon his course in order to arrive. For without such a steady purpose and shortage of imagination, there might seem then no point in going anywhere.

Lone sailors, I have discovered, have many reasons for sailing the oceans. For some it is the challenge, for some the fame, however limited, of doing such a thing. For some it is the feeling that they are better than other men are.

These are people not always easy to stomach when you meet them on the shore. But their attitudes perhaps are needed by them to survive and give a narrow purpose in great waters which tend to overwhelm the mind.

But for all, I think, it is an escape, though not the kind of escape which everyone would choose. It is an escape from the prison of our artificial urban life. An escape to a kingdom where a simple thing can become the whole world and can be conquered by the simple weapons which all of us are born with.

That is why many single-handers feel that they are in some way fulfilling their destiny when they are out there alone on the ocean. For all these feelings were common to men in the hunting childhood of the human race.

There came another spell of light weather with occasional spasms of breeze. This was a good opportunity to do some sail-mending. I was beginning to worry about some of the rips and tears appearing in the sails, especially after the unprepared-for gybes. But the important thing was to keep the

sail-cloth well-fastened to the battens and I spent some time
on a session of wiring up the bamboos. There were still some
twine-bound parts to the sails and these were the areas which
were giving way.

I also did some fishing. I had become thoroughly disil-
lusioned about trade-wind sailing. Before we left, everyone
had something to tell me about sailing in the trades and
everyone mentioned flying fish. Opinion was divided about
how good they were to eat, how many would land on deck,
and whether it paid to encourage them by showing a light so
that I should catch even more. But I used to come away with
the impression that the sea would bear a resemblance to a
marine aerodrome or the view outside a bee-hive in mid-
summer, with busily-flying objects zooming in all directions.
I made a mental note that I would duck as I put my head out
of the hatch in case it was hit by something.

Alas, no speeding flying fish shot past my head. I was not
woken up at dawn by fish flapping on deck, nor did a fish
ever jump into my held-up frying pan. When I arrived in
Barbados I was told that flying fish were out of season. This
does not mean that you were not allowed to shoot them on
the wing, like pheasants, but that they were not there to be
shot.

But in case you are thinking that I had no flying-fish on
deck, you would be wrong. There were dozens. The trouble
was, I did not recognize them for what they were. They were
difficult to see. In each one, with its tiny, delicate wings,
there would have been hardly enough for a sardine's
breakfast, and I could not find enough at any one time to
make a mouthful. These pathetic little creatures would stick
to the deck, or be wedged unseen beneath my stack of
bamboo poles, waiting to be washed off by a wave or by my
bucket about two days later.

So in desperation, I put out an old feather-line I had, and
soon caught a fish. Eagerly I pulled it in to find that it had
taken all the hooks. It was also pumping itself up and down,
like a gasping football, making its spikes stick out like a
pin-cushion. It was a porcupine fish. I had vaguely heard of

such things, but I had made a rule that any fish with spikes or spines on it I would cut away at once. Some of these spines are highly poisonous, and with medical attention so far away, it would not pay to risk such an infection. The single-handed sailor has no-one to get him out of trouble but himself.

There was now a change in the weather, perfect for so long. On the 4th November there was a heavy swell rolling from the north-west as if there was a storm in the direction of Bermuda. That night there were lightning flashes astern out of gathering clouds. I expected squalls at any moment so I was nervous. I did not do much sleeping that night. It was, I remembered for some reason, Guy Fawkes day back home.

The next day the barometer, which had been at 1022-1024 millibars all the way, fell to 1016. My Admiralty Pilot directions stated that a fall of five millibars meant that there was a hurricane on the way. But the wind was light. Although we were in an area where hurricanes could appear, it seemed unlikely. But I worried. That afternoon there was a heavy squall of perhaps force six with some rain. The sky was overcast with heavy, evil-looking black clouds. Then the weather cleared.

From then on I lived with squalls as a permanent nightmare. I soon discounted the hurricane story as a fantasy. By that time the glass had fallen to 1011. Usually during a squall the glass fell. Otherwise it rose. Often it did not move at all. Later I learned to ignore the glass in the tropics.

No squall though, could be ignored. These appeared as great black clouds with black streamers hanging beneath them, or great black lines, like a roll of carpet approaching in the wind. At night these black clouds were blacker than the night itself. From behind these black clouds came calms, or a change of wind, or no change, or rain, or a howling wind squall. There was no way of telling what would happen.

Several times I woke up to find the boat staggering along almost on its beam ends, the water roaring along the deck. Hastily I would leap up to find a strong squall of wind in progress. Then would come the task of shortening sail before the whipping masts split.

On November 9th I actually caught a fish. I was not proud of it. We had been joined by a little group of grey fish with yellow tails. By this time, the boat had begun to acquire a coat of weed and many goose-barnacles. These are strange shell-fish which attach themselves to the bottom of the boat. They are like black rubber tubes with a head of white shell. They seemed to stick out into the water a long way. But perhaps the fish were attracted by this growth on the bottom.

I decided to test out the French lads' harpoon, I loaded the spear and set the elastic. At first the fish darted away, then one came in line. I pressed the trigger and spiked it right through the middle. But unfortunately I could not bring myself to eat it, which was very cowardly. Among the instructions I had had from all sorts of people who claimed to be authorities on eating unknown fish, I was told to avoid those with bright colours. Could this one be described as bright? Certainly the tail was. Eventually I used it as bait on my last hook, and trailed it astern. When I came to pull it in to see what had happened to it, I could feel something nibbling at it. I jerked the line, there was a strong, steady pull, and the line snapped. It must have been a shark.

Later I learned that the fish was a yellow-tailed snapper and good to eat. There was a whole group of them round the boat.

There were several sharks about at the time. Far down underneath the boat so that I could only see them when it was smooth, there was a school of six small sharks, probably nurse sharks. Sometimes I tried to get a line down to them but could never get them interested.

Occasionally a larger one appeared, but not for long. Once, when we were sailing in a smooth swell, a big shark coasted down the slope behind us, turned, and was gone. It seemed to be white with dark patches, like a leopard, but this was perhaps an illusion.

On November 12th I had my first example of another type of squall. A great black line of cloud approached the boat. It looked terrible. I lowered the sails to wait for the violent

Sailing in the Azores with a Portuguese friend. The fields of Fayal are in the background.

Arriving at Horta in the island of Fayal in the Azores. The Portuguese pilot boarded the boat without permission at the harbour entrance, so I insisted upon sailing in, however long it took. The mainsail is looking extremely tattered, with the two top battens broken. In front of the dinghy is the large buoy/fender which I picked up in mid-Atlantic. It was very useful for lying alongside the quay.

On the trip to Spain.
Myself in the cockpit,
with beard.

Myself in the dinghy at
speed. An ever-useful
garden hose was put
round the gunwale to
act as a fender. It was
skulled from the stern
with a paddle. I could
take two passengers in
calm water if no one
breathed. The two
passengers were too
scared to breathe.

wind that must come. The wind changed to the north-east. Then it rained. I have been in rain squalls since, but never as heavy as that. It was so heavy that I instinctively gasped for breath as if I was swimming in the water. From the cockpit I could see only a few feet in either direction, the forward part of the boat being invisible. In a second I was wet through, although without clothes this was not a serious matter. But it was cold, so I went below.

Down below it was like a shower-bath. The cabin-top roof had dried out in the immensely hot sun and the seams had opened up. The water poured in as if there was nothing in the way. Eventually I dug out a waterproof cover and put it over the bunk with myself underneath. It was too late. All the bedding was soaked. I was soaked. Everything was soaked. I lay and shivered, the water pattering on the cover over my ears. Wind I expect and can stand, I thought, but this I can't. I wondered how I was going to make the cabin water-tight.

When the squall was over, it was time to dry out. The bilges were full of water — it had come in through the cabin-top and down through the gaps by the mast-partners. It slopped noisily from one side to the other. The cockpit too was waterlogged, the level having come up to the cockpit floorboards. It took a long time to pump out.

There were other squalls later. But now I felt that we were on the way home. We were on the exact latitude of Barbados, 13° 15′ N, and steering W x N by compass which was true west. I had come to this latitude because it was the safest thing to do if there was likely to be any doubt about my longitude. My radio had taken a soaking during the squall and might not pick up Barbados. Then I should have to sail along the line of the easily found latitude.

There was a snag, though. George, before I left Las Palmas, had warned me of a current off Barbados which was caused by a submarine trench, and tended to push a boat off its latitude. And even this latitude might be difficult to find. Here the southern and northern equatorial currents meet, bringing cloud and sunless conditions. Thus it would be easy to miss Barbados.

15. The Islands

'Miss Barbados? I don't know the girl.'

With this feeble joke, I cheered myself up as I began to look round for signs of land, seaweed, seabirds, anything. There was nothing.

The only birds about were the usual brown creatures which swoop over the waves looking for fish and never seem to rest. Occasionally, there was a whiter bird. But these had been seen almost all the way across, and were no sign of land. As for seaweed, it would all be blown to the west by the trade winds.

I had by this time finished all my books; I had even read through most of Shakespeare. It takes a lot of desperation to do that. I cannot say that I remember much of it, though I actually came to enjoy reading the plays. As for the other books, there is a limit to the number of times you can read the same detective story without eventually grasping what the end is going to be before you have started.

I had several sailing books which I never looked at. Sailing was the last thing I wanted to read about. There were two Saint books, and other extravaganzas, and some travel books. My favourite was Stanley's *Through Darkest Africa*. This entertaining book was perhaps not the most tactful to take on a voyage to the Caribbean.

I used to learn bits of Shakespeare and proclaim them aloud to the winds. *Julius Caesar* was my favourite for this. The idea was not to lose the habit of speaking. This sounds ridiculous, but there is more to say about that later. How much good it did I don't know. No one has yet invited me to become a Shakespearean actor.

The last part of the voyage began to crawl past in an agony of slowness. The wind seemed to be getting more and more fickle with squalls every few hours. Usually these were of the wind-robbing type which left *Erik* bobbing helplessly in the swell with the sails flapping about. And even with a good wind, he seemed to be going very slowly through the water. This was not imagination. All the time in the warm water goose barnacles were attaching themselves to the hull. On the starboard side out of the sun, these extended well up above the water-line, dipping into the ocean when the yacht rolled. Lying below in my bunk I could hear the increased noise from the water as it trickled past these animals.

On the night of the 16th November, thirty days out from Las Palmas, the Barbados broadcasting service came through loud and clear, and right on the bow when I twisted the radio about to find the direction. That was a good sign. Although the radio could not give any idea of how far away the island was, I was now able to find out the correct Greenwich time. With the aid of this, I could plot my position the following noon. It was 13° 15′ N, 58° 43′ W. Bang on line, and fifty miles to go!

At 11.30 that night, there was a glow in the sky ahead. That meant a town — Bridgetown, Barbados. Knowing that I should have a strenuous day making the land, I retired below for a sleep. I was woken up at two in the morning by a flapping, thumping noise. For a moment I lay puzzled, wondering what it was. Then I realized. I rushed on deck and collected my first good-sized edible flying fish. It still fluttered in my hand. I looked at the now bright glow in the sky, and threw it back into the sea. There would be no chance to eat it. But at least I had had a flying fish.

By dawn, the curious eastern lighthouse of Barbados, flashing once every 120 seconds, like a Red Indian putting a blanket on a fire, vanished into the daylight and we headed for Southern Point. A black Barbadian in a fast sailing catamaran came soaring up and swooped round us. Then past the houses along the beach to Carlisle Bay.

The sight was amazing, and I could not believe my eyes. The water turned to white, the colour of the white sand, and, at first, I thought we were running aground, until I saw that all the boats, quite large ones too, were sitting on this sand. The water was so clear that it seemed transparent. After the murky northern seas, it was an extraordinary sight.

Slowly and painfully, we tacked into the shore. The sails had worked well enough down wind, but now they were so tattered and torn that we could barely make up to the anchorage. The foul bottom did not help either.

Then I saw George in his little boat. He had just had a visit from the Customs. He showed me where to anchor and sent the Customs man straight on to me, which saved a lot of hanging about.

Wanderbird of Devon was there too, and Ian and Brownie gave me a great welcome. Obviously, I had not forgotten how to speak to people. Later they told me that they had not wanted to mention it at the time, but for half-an-hour I was almost incoherent, though I had not known it. But it was like coming home.

What an extraordinary thing it is to do, to want to cross the Atlantic! That you always knew. But in some strange way you were sustained by the fact that the thing was so extraordinary and seemed impossible.

But what, when you have done it, what then?

At first, there is a feeling of disbelief. The boat sits mirrored in the warm blue waters of tropical paradise. He seems to float in a cloud of unreality and so makes your arrival too seem quite unreal. You swim, and bask in the hot sun to try and fill your senses with the knowledge that you have arrived at last, but still it does not really sink in. So many times, when things have seemed to go too well, then you have tempered your enthusiasm.

'Don't get too pleased!', you say severely to yourself. 'Or you'll get something you aren't expecting.'

So even in an hour of success, the spectre of possible failure at some future time forever haunts the scene.

Now, you realize cautiously that there is no future failure.

How hard it is to win when you have been for so long struggling not to lose! Triumph is something that must be shrugged on like a shirt, an artificial ornament to clothe success.

Then, after triumph, creep in those nasty, niggling thoughts.

'Was this so great a thing to do? Was it important enough to make all those sacrifices worth while?'

When you have staked a lot of future life upon a future goal, then that goal had better seem important when it is won. That is why many in achievement cling hard to the thing they have achieved. But there are others who find themselves cast down in disillusionment. . . .

Now, too, is the time to think what you must do after this. Having achieved the aim of sailing across an ocean, can you really be content in the same old way to cruise to other goals? What life could be more pleasant? Yet that very goad which made you come is now at work to make you go. For there are fresh worlds to conquer, many more demanding than an easy life of adventure. Having made a voyage into unknown dangers, perhaps it is time to plunge into the life which most of us know, and see what you can do. . . .

It just shows that we are never satisfied.

Strangely, having come across the Atlantic by the easy route, sensibly chosen as the easiest, I now felt that this had been too easy. Perhaps I would not feel that I had really crossed the Atlantic unless I sailed back again as well. . . .

First, though, I had to enjoy the West Indies.

Barbados was a marvellous place to arrive at. We had full use of the somewhat exclusive Yacht Club and were made at home. The Rotary Club were marvellous. I was invited to a lunch where we heard the Leader of the Opposition give a talk on 'The Value of Having an Opposition'. It seemed very sensible of him.

Hospitality was overwhelmingly embarrassing. After a week of this, and repairing my sails, I knew I had to go on. I was now running short of money and the plan was to go to

Grenada and get work on a charter yacht if I could.

The trip to Grenada seemed an anti-climax. In the end, it took three days, there being hardly any wind. Because of the calms, I decided to go round the southern end of the island, thus keeping to windward of it. This was a mistake. No-one in the Islands sails to windward of the islands, I discovered. Even in calms, there is likely to be more wind under the lee side, due to land effects.

On the third night, I rounded Point Saline. There was a nasty moment when I was being dragged backwards in almost calm conditions towards the rocks. It was an adverse tide, quite unmentioned on my chart. I had to drop the kedge anchor, and it was a strain to remember where it had been stowed. But that day, I was coming into St. George's. I was given a tow in through the cut into the lagoon where yachts lie. I should never have been able to sail in.

Having taken so long to get to Grenada, I had arrived on a Sunday and had to pay three pounds in overtime to the customs for the privilege, and for harbour dues. It was the only place I paid anything on the whole voyage.

Grenada I did not like. It is a beautiful island, one of the best endowed with bays and beaches. The atmosphere, however, is brooding, perhaps because it is high and lush. Dark stories abounded of a political dictatorship, the secret police known as The Mongoose, and troubles white people have with the authorities. It was reputed to be impossible to get work in the charter boats except as a crew going to sea. The charter-boat skippers themselves were miserable. They had had a disastrous two seasons because of an American slump, combined with a tourist scare over Black Power demonstrations. Business dropped off completely.

I was forced to get work on one of those boats, standing in for a West Indian lad who had deserted. For this, I was paid fifty West Indian dollars, or ten pounds a week for a month, including paying someone to look after *Erik*. We sailed with charterers through the islands as far as St. Vincent, visiting all the beautiful Grenadines. It could have been enjoyable and interesting. It was interesting, but I did not enjoy it.

With some money in my pocket, I could now stock up with stores which were otherwise getting low. I had time, too, to do some work on the boat.

The cabin top was painted in an effort to keep the water out. The cabin had had to be thoroughly cleaned out when I had come back from my charter work, since everything in it was covered in mildew. In the damper parts of the lining of the waterproof covers, little maggots squirmed and crawled. The mattress coverings had to be thrown away.

By the time I left, the bottom of the boat looked as if it might be foul. There was no way of dealing with this in St. George's Harbour, however. The water was absolutely thick. Opinions varied about what would happen if one tried to swim under the boat to clean the fouling off. There were reputed to be barracuda, poisonous waste from the slip where yachts were cleaned off, and sewage. No-one had ever been seen to swim in the water. But perhaps that was because it was against the law.

I had, by this time, decided to go to Antigua. This was the other charter centre and it was said that it might be easier to get work there. At any rate, I was fed up with Grenada.

All that was needed now was a supply of bamboos. Although these grow in the island, it was not possible to buy them anywhere. Eventually, I was directed to the zoo. Here I was ushered to the director. He listened carefully to my story.

'I think we can do something for you,' he said. 'We have men going up into the island. I'll get them to cut some bamboos for you when they're up there. Today is Friday. Come on Monday afternoon, and I'll have them ready for you.'

On Monday afternoon, I arrived and was shown into his office.

'You're late,' he told me. 'I said Monday morning.'

I was surprised.

'I'm sorry, I thought you said Monday afternoon.'

'No,' he said. 'Monday morning. I was expecting you this morning.'

Then I understood. No money was expected, but payment was.

'I'm very sorry,' I told him. 'I must have made a mistake. I'm sorry if I've put you out. You must be busy.'

He looked at me for a moment, then he beamed.

'I've got them,' he said, and pointed to a bundle of bamboos standing in the corner.

'They're marvellous,' I enthused. 'Just what I wanted. Thank you very much.'

And off I went with my bamboos. It was very nice of him.

While making these preparations to leave Granada, life there began to pall. It was enlivened only by Charlie.

'Who's Charlie? Everyone knows Charlie.'

And everyone in Grenada seemed to. Charlie had arrived in a yacht two years before. He and a partner ran a catamaran taking people for sailing trips off Grand Anse. One night, the catamaran blew ashore ending up a total wreck.

I had met Charlie the first night in Grenada, on board the yacht whose owner had given me a tow. He was a small man with a beard and a merry face. He told me he was forty, though he looked much less.

'Are you prejudiced?' he asked me almost at once, when we were talking about the West Indians. 'Well, if you aren't, you soon will be.'

I never knew whether to take him seriously. He got along with the locals better than anyone. Often he would yell to me from the cafe bar where the fishermen drank, as I walked up the road back from town.

'Come and have a drink,' he would shout. 'I can't stay sober all day.'

Already, he looked three-quarters gone. Then we would spend an hour or two knocking back rum in the West Indian style — a sip of rum washed down with water from a mug. Sometimes, the mug was cleaned. It was a good way of getting to know the fishermen. They were nearly always there. Charlie told me about their fishing methods.

'Not many of them run their own boats,' he said. 'A man will own several boats and then let them out to fishermen in return for half the catch. Maybe that's why they don't work so hard. Enough rum and food for tomorrow is all they want. There's plenty of fish about here. Sometimes a big shoal will come and they'll go out and get a good catch. They sell it for a good price and then come here and drink rum. For three days they drink rum, while that shoal sits outside the harbour. Then, when they run out of money, they go out and the shoal's gone. "Fishing no good", they say, "There no fish about".'

A fisherman called Herman and wearing a crumpled hat shuffled to us over the dusty floor.

'Buy us a drink, Charlie,' he said.

'I've got no money,' said Charlie. 'I want one from you.'

Herman bought us all red rum in a little bottle. We took it in turns to pour a little into a glass, take a mouthful and wash it down with the mug of water.

'That's the West Indian way to drink,' Charlie said. 'They're a good lot here. That's because when I've got money I buy them drinks. Now I haven't got any. They know that.'

Charlie believed in making his own entertainment. That was why it was amusing to spend an evening in the town with him.

'Remember,' says Charlie, 'if anyone asks you, you haven't seen me. I'm not supposed to be here in the island.'

A van drives past. A bellow comes from the driving seat, 'Hi, Charlie!'.

'You haven't seen me,' continues Charlie. 'Let's go in here.'

We go inside a dingy bar. It is really a shop. A young woman in glasses stands behind the counter.

'Here she is!' Charlie shouts. 'Here's my girl friend. Let's have a drink, darling.'

Severely, she pours us out a rum. He seems suddenly drunk. 'She's the one for me,' he says. 'Have you got a husband?'

'Yes, Charlie.'

'Have you got a boyfriend, too?'

'No, Charlie. You be quiet, Charlie.'

'Of course, you've got a boyfriend,' he bellows. 'I'm your boyfriend. You know, there's only one man I hate in this town. That's your husband.'

There is laughter in the bar. Her husband, standing quietly at the end of the bar, is pointed out to him.

'I hate you,' Charlie shouts. 'You know why. Because you're the husband of my girl-friend.'

He looks embarrassed, not knowing whether to be proud or angry. She says:

'Hush, Charlie. I don't know you, Charlie.'

The husband says, 'Have a drink with me, Charlie.'

'No,' shouts Charlie, 'I'm getting *you* a drink. You know why? Because you're the husband of the girl I love.'

After a drink and laughter, we go out into the street where the lights twinkle in the black water of the harbour.

'Let's go to Long John's,' he says.

Silva is a sallow Portuguese and runs a bar. The local wits call him 'Long John' Silva. There is a new barmaid in Long John's. She is young and very beautiful, as the occasional girl from Grenada can be.

'This bar's the most expensive in Grenada,' Charlie says loudly, 'but Long John's my best friend. Introduce me to your new barmaid, Long John.'

Long John's smile fades for a moment, then revives.

'This is Olive. Olive, you know Charlie? Everyone knows Charlie.'

She shakes her head. She is shy. I take my cue.

'Surely you know Charlie. Everyone knows Charlie.'

'No, I don't know him.'

Charlie nudges me. He seems far gone.

'Isn't she beautiful? Isn't she a beautiful girl? She the one I'm going to have for my girl-friend. Do you smoke, Olive?'

'No, Charlie.'

'Do you drink?'

'No, Charlie.'

'Do you make love?'

'No, Charlie.'

She laughs and the ice is broken. Now she knows Charlie.

The next evening her boy friend is at the end of the bar, silently drinking. He has heard about Charlie and he lives in the West Indies. Olive must be watched. Easy living is not always easy.

But now Charlie is having an argument with someone. They wager the next round of drinks and the other man loses. He says it's not fair, and goes out, but Charlie orders the drinks, regardless.

Over this, there is a tremendous row. Long John says that Charlie ordered the drinks, so he must pay. Charlie refuses. Long John's smile slips. He threatens to call the police. I pay and drag Charlie away.

'Let's go to Chinatown,' Charlie says.

Chinatown is just a collection of open air kiosk-bars. The roofs look something like those on Chinese pagodas, hence the name, Chinatown.

It is crowded tonight. The navy is in. We make for the most crowded kiosk. Herman the fisherman staggers up and I remember him by his hat. He always wears the same hat. He is drunk and can hardly speak. He takes my hand and shakes it.

'Herman, you're drunk,' slurs Charlie. A night time girl hears him and turns delightedly.

'It's Charlie,' she cries. She has her arm round a young navy lad who looks drunk and bemused. Occasionally, she strokes him absent-mindedly in a motherly fashion. Her attention is on Charlie.

'He's Jesus, you're Judas.'

She has obviously seen a religious film where two of the characters bear a close resemblance to our bearded figures. West Indians are keen on religion. She is obsessed with her private joke.

'He's Jesus, you're Judas. Charlie, he's Jesus, you're Judas.'

She tries to fix me with her eye to show interest, but her gaze drunkenly falls to the ground. Charlie puts his fist against her body. She thrusts against it several times and laughs.

'Not tonight, Charlie. I've got someone tonight. I'm busy.'

She looks at him with obvious affection. Herman insists on buying me a drink. I refuse. He insists, and I settle for a Coca-Cola, which is the cheapest. Then I buy him another rum. It is the final straw. Before, he was drunk. Now, he is paralytic. He collapses, motionless, onto the ground.

When the bar is closed, we leave. Charlie is not as drunk as he seems, and he tells me the philosophy which has enabled him to survive here for two years.

'You've got to jolly these people along,' he says. 'Then they'll like you. I bought them all drinks to start with. Now they'll do anything for me. They know me.'

I realize that Charlie, like all characters, is really a professional actor. Grenada is his stage. But no actor could have got through better to his audience.

We get a lift back by standing in the middle of the road to stop any vehicle which comes along. The first driver does not know Charlie. He tries to charge us a dollar, thinking that we are tourists. 'No, thank you,' we say, getting out again.

The next driver knows Charlie and gives us a lift. Another performance is over.

'There's nothing to do here,' a West Indian told me, mournfully, 'but drink and make love.'

Although it was mid-winter, the lagoon was very hot; it was surrounded by high hills and the cooling trade winds could not touch it. At night, the air was loud with the chirp of crickets and the bell-like song of tiny frogs, little bigger than the end joint of a finger. A steel band would sometimes play, its noise echoing round the lagoon, practising the same tune hour after hour. On the slopes above the isolated lights of houses would shine through the palm trees high up towards the stars.

Grenada is beautiful. I was in the end sorry to leave. The anchor chain, as I pulled it up, was foul, the top part being smothered with weed, the bottom with mud. It stank for ages. We headed through the narrow cut, and out of the harbour towards the clean and empty sea.

16. Antigua

The voyage to Antigua was not one of our most successful. My plan was to put into Martinique, which, I was told, I must certainly visit.

The passage along the lee side of Grenada was slow. Off-shore, in the lee of the islands, it is usually calm; but right under the land there is always some wind. It comes rolling down the hills, noticeably cooler than the air around. Down the valleys there are often strong gusts, while under the headlands, the wind drops light. All sailing along the islands is done on the lee sides. On the eastern sides, where the trade winds always blow, there are reefs which lie some distance offshore, while the western sides are usually clear. In addition, the current slackens off under the islands, and you are sheltered from the trades, which often blow very strongly, up to force six which is too much for comfort in a small boat.

Between the islands, a dash must be made to the lee of the next islands. Some of these channels are very rough, the wind and current being funnelled by the land.

We made slowly along the coast of Grenada, making use of the occasional gust of wind. We were rather further off-shore than necessary, since I had no-one to keep watch if I wanted a rest. There were several boats passing in-shore. An American yacht overhauled us easily. They had plenty of canvas set. As they passed, they hurled a bottle of beer at me. It fell in the water. They threw another and it struck the sail and clunked into the cockpit. It was ice cold, I waved gratefully.

Under the deep green of the high land, so close that it looked as if it was crawling along the shore, crept a native schooner. These all have engines now, but usually the sails are set too. They have very low schooner rigs and are designed so that they can be careened or pulled over on one side in the water. The weed can then be scraped off and anti-fouling put on to combat teredo worm. They are gradually disappearing. There is a high loss rate and some of the skippers are dishonest, which does not improve their trading business.

As we left the lee of the island, the wind increased. Night fell. The wind was now almost north-east, entirely unsuitable for a trip to the north, and was increasing all the time, kicking up a choppy sea. *Erik* was going extremely slowly, due, I suspected, to the fouling on the bottom. When it was light, I resolved to have a look at it. We were not making much better than two knots as the boat see-sawed into the waves.

The next day, we were out of sight of land, which was obviously many miles to the east. We were well out of any shipping here, whereas if we had hopped from island to island in the usual way, I should have had to watch out at night. Some of the native schooners never carried lights. I had a look at the bottom of the boat. It was a staggering sight. It was completely covered with barnacles, some on top of others, and looked as smooth as a hair brush. I tried to scrape some off with the dinghy paddle as we moved along.

It was impossible to make up to Martinique since the wind dropped under the land and the boat would not move against it. Regretfully, I abandoned the attempt and set off towards Antigua. It took five days to do the three hundred miles from Grenada to St. John's Harbour, Antigua. Here they were politely astonished at my appearance.

'You've come all the way from Grenada, in *that*?', the Customs man said, as he stamped my passport. The stamp gave me leave to stay in Antigua for a week, provided that I did not work on the island.

I soon discovered that there was nothing at St. John's. I had hoped to buy some tools and equipment I needed there before going to English Harbour where nearly all the yachts went. But I soon gave this up, and set off for English Harbour. The wind dropped off, so this voyage again took a long time. But I did not mind. Antigua has one of the most beautiful of coast-lines.

My entrance into English Harbour was spectacular, since I got a rope mooring line caught between the keel and the rudder. The boat came to an abrupt standstill until I was helped by a character in a dinghy who towed me to my anchorage. He was the mate on a yacht owned by a rich Frenchman. I was invited on board later and presented with a self-inflating rubber dinghy, which he was scrapping.

Harry and Elizabeth of the *Zotty* were there, moored to the˙ quay not far away from us. When I went over to see them, Harry said:

'You're looking for work? It's a pity you weren't here before Christmas, I had more work then than I could handle.'

As a former trained electronics engineer, he had been asked to repair all sorts of equipment from radar sets to generators. I could not see how I could help, not knowing a thing about such matters, until he explained what had happened on their voyage across.

Three days out from Las Palmas, Harry slipped a disc in his back. He spent the rest of the trip lying on his back, living on brandy and aspirins.

'He looks like an inmate of Belsen,' Elizabeth said.

She had done everything on the boat, including the navigation, directed by Harry from his bunk. It was almost a single-handed voyage. It was a tribute to the careful preparations they had made for ease of handling.

Harry had begun to work under protest, since his back was not yet recovered, but it appeared that there was no-one there who was capable of doing electrical or mechanical repairs in a reasonable time and at a reasonable price. He had started by helping people to connect up their electrical equipment to the shore supply which was, as they say, in a shocking state, charging only for the time spent. Then he had been asked to mend other things. Because of his accident and the fact that many of these jobs required lifting heavy equipment, I was enrolled to help him. Eventually, there were four of us employed on various tasks about the dockyard.

Besides Harry, there was John, an Englishman. He had a yacht called *Solan Goose*, was an electronics design engineer, and a very clever fellow. There was Alan, a Danish lad, who was an electrician, and a very ingenious fellow. And there was myself, who was a nothing, and a very practised liar. For I am proud to say that I became the Honda generator expert. I had never even seen one before, but they only needed their engines tuning, and we promised no charge for failures. Perhaps as a result, we seldom had one. By these means, I somehow was able to stay in the Caribbean until the summer season, when it was time to go back to England.

For many, life on a yacht in the Caribbean is ideal. Most of those based there are engaged in charter work. It is not ideal for those who are interested in the actual sailing of a boat. Most of the charterers are delighted with the idea of sailing in a yacht in the Caribbean, but they soon find that the winds and waves of the seas there are very rugged. Thus, most charter yachts are simply floating hotels with sails hung up as a decoration. The real business is swimming, snorkelling and acquiring a tan.

The weather in the Caribbean in winter is marvellous. Life is lived out of doors with the minimum of clothing and windows tend not to have glass in them. In a yacht it was easy to live cheaply, for there were no dues for lying at anchor, and the police officials were helpful and courteous — except for one, whom we named the Little Corporal.

One day friends in an ex-Baltic Trader next door brought their dog ashore. They had been forbidden to do this. The Little Corporal appeared:

'If that dog doesn't go back, I'll shoot it,' he said. He produced a gun from his pocket and started to fiddle with it, trying to get bullets into the magazine.

'Those things can kill people, you know,' someone said, at this inept and dangerous performance. We started to mutter

The method of reefing. The mainsail halyard has been slackened off so that part of the sail is taken up in the lifts. To prevent the sheet from being too long, it was shortened by hauling in on one end and a knot tied in it. Once this adjustment was made, the sail was controlled by the main part of the sheet in the usual manner. The boat is sailing himself with the helm lashed. It pays not to fall overboard at such a time.

Sailing with the main reefed. You can sail with as much or as little of the sail up as you like.

Sailing at Horta, Fayal, in the Azores, with the town and harbour in the background. There are spare bamboos on the side-deck and a fender is still hanging over near the stern. The sails have been patched up. The thin line from the peak of the mainsail to the batten below was to help take the strain of the uppermost sheet.

Myself sailing *Erik the Red*.

about the Tontons Macoutes of Haiti and police states, and
he was shamed into putting it away.

Sometimes, the police would conduct searches of the boats
for drugs, in the belief that drugs were coming ashore from
the yachts. Undoubtedly some were, but it was nothing to
the amount that was on the island already. One character
offered to sell me marijuana, saying he grew his own.

'There are fields of the stuff in Antigua,' he told me, 'But
the police here don't know what it looks like.'

Certainly, it might have been tempting for yachts to
smuggle marijuana, since it was very difficult to get work in
the islands. There had been one visitation to most of the
British islands by Black Power leaders, who had stirred up
anti-white sentiment. When I arrived in Antigua, there was an
election in progress, the new and rising party promising to
remove all white people, including tourists. To their surprise,
they got in and had to abandon this unworkable and suicidal
policy. To appease the voters, they began to clamp down on
white people living in the island by refusing work-permits to
many non-Antiguans. This would have been sensible had they
not needed these people.

All this affected English Harbour surprisingly little. It was
a world of its own. The major interest seemed to be in the
personal lives of the community. Conduct in the charter
fraternity tended to be very free and easy. Many charter
skippers made a point of getting the most attractive or willing
girl they could, regardless of cooking ability. Sometimes a
skipper and wife will both work at chartering, the skipper
taking on a cook, and the wife going to work as cook on
another charter yacht. In a part of the world where living is
easy, standards do not have to be so strict.

For a white person, it is always possible to get a job in
English Harbour, or else a passage out to the States, on to
Panama and Australia, or back to Europe. Skippers of the
charter yachts will go to any lengths to avoid hiring West
Indian crews. This is in spite of the fact that West Indians do
not expect such high wages as the white people from richer
countries. It is not solely due to colour prejudice. Those

charterers who are prejudiced do not mind seeing a black crew; it is part of the scene. Unfortunately, many islanders do not make good crews, often deserting yachts in the middle of a charter. They have got themselves a bad reputation as a result.

Other ways of making money depend upon some initiative. For instance, Harry might say to me:

'There's a yacht over there which wants the weed scraping off its bottom. They say they can't afford to get the boat slipped. It might be worth a few dollars to you.'

It is plain that to clean the boat while it is still in the water entails some sort of diving equipment. The local skin-diver has been approached and has asked too much money. I go to fetch John, as one of the firm. I know an American who has a motor-powered air-pump, complete with diving masks. This we borrow under some pretext, and practise with so that we can appear with great confidence and efficiency to clean the boat.

All this was good fun and helped to give a spice to the stay in Antigua. Eventually, though, things turned sour. There were all sorts of feuds and rivalries in the dockyard, and some of these came to the boil. I was glad when I had made enough money to last me, so I hoped, until I got back to England. I was able to retire.

This money business, I discovered, was the major problem for most of the sea-faring crowd. Living on a boat is cheap, but it is not always so easy to work one's way round the world. These are the days of work-permits, and anyone planning a voyage without some sort of income, must plot his passage by the countries where he can get work. Those who have valuable skills are in the best position, especially if these are of the sort useful for yacht repairs. Some people manage to get work on land and will stay in the same port for a year, earning enough for the next leg of the voyage.

Yacht people are like gypsies in many ways. They may stay for a time in one place, but eventually they must move on. When you meet people from another yacht, they, or you, will say, 'Do you know so and so?' You will always know someone in common, or have some news about a yacht you have met.

I did not feel that I had seen many of the islands, so I was pleased when John and Anne on *Solan Goose*, invited me to go on a cruise with them south. John was the electronics expert of the firm and Anne was his wife. With us came Herta, who was Danish. Her skipper had left her to look after his yacht while he went and worked for an oil-company in Pakistan. We cruised as far as Martinique, visiting many beautiful places. Cruising with company is far more fun, I decided. It was a good holiday.

It was now time to get *Erik* ready for the return voyage to England. Whenever I told anyone that I was going back to England, they would look at me in astonishment.

'Whatever for?', they would say, wide-eyed. 'The journey back again is quite a different thing, you know. It's much harder than coming across.'

Perhaps it was this point that made me decide to go back to England. The journey across had, indeed, been easy. I had already met someone who had twice sailed across in ordinary open fishing-boats, without any public acclaim. It was plain that the whole business had been highly exaggerated by many people. Would the journey back be any different? It would be interesting to find out.

The first task was to clean off the bottom of the boat. I decided to do this at once, since Antigua Race Week was due soon. Contrary to what one might expect from the title, this was not a week devoted to demonstrations of negro solidarity, but a regatta. Although I would obviously be last in every race, it seemed that it might be fun to take part. I could not afford to get the boat slipped, so I studied the tide situation. I discovered that this should be enough to uncover all the wooden part of the hull, which could then be painted to help keep out teredo worm. The boat had not been painted for nine months and I was beginning to worry about this pest.

The beaching was not successful. Even though the water looked completely flat, there was a slight surge. It was enough to wash the sand away from beneath the keel. Hidden underneath was coral rock. The keel began to bang heavily upon it. Before the boat had settled, a chunk several inches long had been knocked off the after end of the keel, revealing the steel reinforcement. To make matters worse, the pounding was directly underneath the rudder. The next thing I saw was the rudder hanging on by one pintle, while the other two, I discovered, had been shaken free from the sockets into which they were welded, and had simply fallen out. Perhaps it was a good thing they had done it now, instead of later, half-way across the Atlantic.

With help, I got the boat off the beach. It was plainly no use trying to paint it. I made do, by scraping the bottom, swimming under the boat. Even in those warm waters, it was hard work. The rudder, I was glad to find, was not too badly damaged. But, I noticed that teredo worm had got into the bottom of it, leaving a gap where the wood had been eaten away. I hoped that they had not made their way into the hull, but there was now no way of telling.

The pintles were easy to mend. Fortunately, I had designed them so that they would be easy for our village blacksmith to make without complicated drawings, so that they were somewhat rudimentary. I salvaged two bolts of the right diameter, sawed them the right length, and pushed them into the sockets. I now had simple-to-obtain, replaceable pintles. I should have thought of that in the first place.

After Race Week, in which there was actually a race in which we didn't come last, being last but one, *Erik*'s sails were looking very much the worse for wear. It was plainly touch-and-go whether they would last across the Atlantic for a second time. However, one of the charter skippers kindly gave me a very large cotton Genoa which had split. I laid it out on the quay, put the old sails over it, and cut round them. The battens were then fixed to the sails and the edges sewn, with huge stitches to save time. Friends also sat down gallantly and sewed. This explained the appearance of smaller stitches. I had previously cut down the length of the battens in the old sail, so that the leeches of the sails went perpendicular. It made the sails easier to handle when tacking.

The only thing I was short of now was a radio. My little transistor had finally ceased to function, being many years old. To replace it, Herta gave me a Hitachi radio, which they themselves had been given. Some wires were broken, but John, the electronics expert, mended it for me so that it was as good as new. It was ten times better than my old one, having two short wave bands, a medium wave band, and a long wave band with directional aerial.

Soon it was time to be off. The hurricane season was fast approaching. In company with *Zotty*, we went for a final holiday to Green Island, a beautiful and isolated part of Antigua, and explored inland. At one cane-cutting village, we were followed everywhere by the children, who had never seen such scantily dressed white apparitions before. When we stopped at a shop for the inevitable Coca-Cola, they gathered round the doorway, staring at us, perhaps twenty of them. The woman told them to go away.

'There's no need to stare at them like that,' she said. 'Just because we're black and they're coloured.'

We realized the danger of judging the people of the islands by the relatively sophisticated workers for the tourist trade.

The reef-sheltered bay was beautiful. Over shallow reefs great parrot-fish a yard long stuck their tails out of the water to eat the coral. On the outer reefs, the sea thundered. It was just the trip to make me feel what I was missing now that it was time to leave.

17. To Bermuda

There is a part of the North Atlantic known to those who have to use it as the Dreaded Triangle. It includes Florida and Bermuda. Over these sunny seas the elements can conspire on occasions to catch the unwary. Along the coast of America and eastward across the Atlantic goes the Gulf Stream, making four knots at times. This, combined with a northerly gale can produce the most vicious of wind-against-current effects. Here, too, is a part prone to hurricanes. Wherever they start, most will travel somewhere over this area. Perhaps other things happen too, which no-one knows about. Even aeroplanes have disappeared in those parts, vanishing without trace.

Early summer, though, was the best time to go and I expected no trouble. But I wanted to be clear of Bermuda by the beginning of July, when the occasional tropical storm occurs.

We sailed out through the entrance of English Harbour on the 14th June, 1971. According to my log book, at the time it was the 7th June. On this hangs a story.

It was sad to be leaving. English Harbour is one of the most pleasant and safest of anchorages. It is virtually unspoilt, and of great historical interest. It was a little community with its own social life, men going off with each others' wives, fights, quarrels, parties, all the things which happen in any other community. It was like leaving home. We squeezed out of the entrance and the green slopes began to recede. We were travelling along the island on a course to clear Cade's Reef, and pass to westward of Antigua.

SELF-STEERING

METHOD No. 1

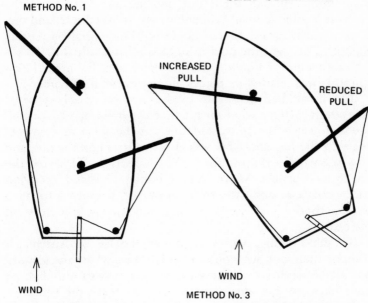

INCREASED PULL

REDUCED PULL

WIND

WIND

METHOD No. 3

METHOD No. 2

SHEET LINES ATTACHED TO TILLER WITH SLIPPERY HITCH.

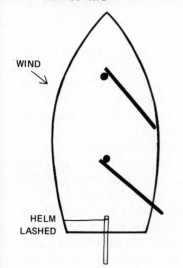

WIND

HELM LASHED

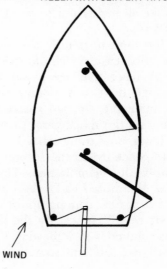

WIND

One hour out of harbour — and one of the battens in the main broke. It had dried out and become brittle and the pressure of the new sail broke it across. It was the second one down, which meant that it could not be ignored by reefing the sail. I brought the boat head to wind and fished it. This is a fancy name for binding another piece over the break like a splint. It was secured by pieces of my never-failing wire.

The break had been due to the method of self-steering. The south-easterly wind meant that the main had to be well round towards the bow, and this put the sheet at a narrow angle to the battens. This was always a strain on the sail, and now the wind was up to force five on occasion. I lowered the sail by two panels. As we were rounding the island, the wind had come dead upon the stern. However, I resolved to try a new method of self-steering when the wind was slightly on the beam.

By the evening, we were under the lee of Antigua. I realized that soon we would be in latitudes where the sun did not set between six and seven every night, with only half an hour between day and night. I now set upon the routine I had resolved to follow all the way back where shipping would be more frequent than the way across. The plan was to keep awake all night, and to sleep by day. This first night was not difficult.

By noon next day, the wind had come round slightly to the north-east, which put the wind on the beam. It was fresh, being force five. We passed St. Kitts, and St. Marten with Anguilla next to it looking like a sand-bank, and Dog Island. By midnight, we had passed Sombrero, a small island with room for not much more than a light-house.

I was now using what I called Self-steering Gear Number Two, since it was the second most frequently used. This was simply the helm lashed. The more the wind came off the bow, the more I had to let out the mizen to balance the helm and stop *Erik* coming up into the wind. Altering the mainsail made no difference. By the time the wind was on the beam, this method was somewhat unreliable. The mizen had to be eased well off and sometimes, if the wind dropped a little,

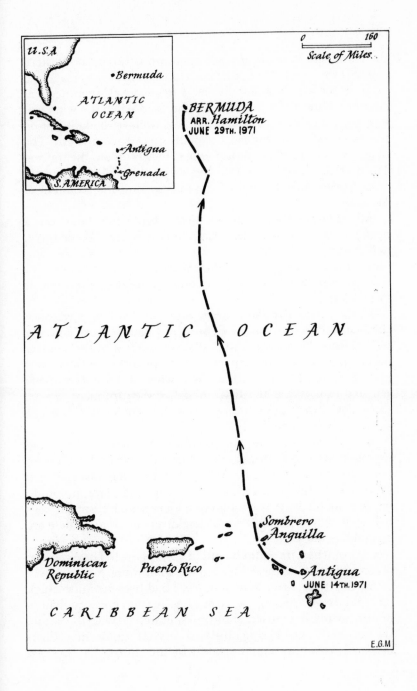

Inset map:
U.S.A
•Bermuda
ATLANTIC
OCEAN
•Antigua
Grenada
S.AMERICA

0   160
Scale of Miles.

BERMUDA
ARR. *Hamilton*
JUNE 29TH. 1971

ATLANTIC   OCEAN

Sombrero
Anguilla

Dominican
Republic   Puerto Rico

Antigua
JUNE 14TH. 1971

CARIBBEAN   SEA

E.G.M

there was not enough leverage from the sail to push the stern towards the wind. Then the boat would gybe.

To cater for these conditions, I devised Self-steering Gear Number Three, which could also be used when the wind was nearly on the stern. This method was to have the sails out on the same side, but to lead the main sheet to windward. The main was sheeted in rather more tightly than the mizen. Thus, if the boat came into the wind, the pull on the main would overcome the pull of the mizen, and *Erik* would head off again.

All these self-steering methods kept the boat on a dead-straight course under nearly all conditions. Of the three, Self-steering Gear Number Two was undoubtedly the simplest and the best. On another voyage, I would arrange to have a rig so that this method could be used all the time. It can be done.

For the next five days, there were good winds, always on the beam. Progress was good, but this I had to guess. The sky was continually overcast, so that getting a shot of the sun was impossible. Very little happened to disturb the routine. I was pulling a book out of the shelf when a huge cockroach scuttled out. It was the first one I had seen for many weeks, since any insect or crawling thing on the boat I used to slaughter quite mercilessly.

'There's no room on this boat for you and me,' I would say, and spray it with my aerosol can of insect killer. It is no good trying to swat a cockroach. In the first place, it can move faster than you can, and in the second place, if you do happen to hit it, it is cunningly designed to jettison its eggs before it dies. Thus, instead of one dead cockroach, there are several live ones.

Cockroaches are entirely suited for survival. They can live on anything, or, if there isn't anything, nothing.

By this time, after long practice, I had become quite quick on the draw. Seizing my can, I gave the creature half a minute while it scurried about, desperately trying to escape. It vanished and I congratulated myself upon my killer-instinct. Now the boat was clear of the things. Later, I saw another, but this one got away. Or perhaps it was the same one, and is still there yet. Life at sea is made up of such small things.

On the fourth day, I decided it was time to do some fishing. I had bought some large hooks, and a friend had given me some nylon and steel traces which, he said, could catch a fifty pound fish. I put a piece of multi-coloured towel on the hook and towed it astern.

In no time at all, I had caught a huge clump of Sargasso weed. There seemed little point in towing this behind the boat, so I had to give up fishing. The weed was floating in the water. It was pale brown and often had small shell-fish living in it. It did not cling together, as it was supposed to do, but when the breeze was light, it would collect in long windrows, like rows of hay in a field. We would glide into these big patches like an icebreaker in brown ice, the boat would check and then we would pass through. Down below in my bunk I could hear the swishing as we continually passed through the weed.

The sixth and seventh days were calm. The water lay like grass under a still-cloudy sky. At night, sheet lightning flickered to the north, and flashed reflections into the water. After the clear skies of the trade winds, not to see the stars at night, or the billowy clouds racing along with the wind by day gave me a strange muffled feeling. But the strong beam winds of the past few days had been uncomfortable and wearing. A calm was pleasant and restful.

All this time, I had been navigating by dead reckoning since the sky was so overcast. This was simply another name for guesswork in my case. Every four hours, or when anything happened, I used to put in my exercise-book 'log' the time, course and speed I guessed we were making. These speeds would be added up, and the courses averaged out, and an estimate of the position put on the chart every day. There was no need for this to be exact, so far from land. Besides, I had no speedometer or patent log for giving the exact distance run. That day was bright and sunny in the morning, so I was able to get an exact latitude and longtitude, 25°

48′ N, 64° 13′ W. My distance run, based on guessed-at speeds put me at a latitude of 25° 50′ N. I crowed over this for a while. At that time, I did not realize the mistake I was making. But it meant that, out of the nine hundred odd miles to Bermuda, we had only four hundred to do.

That afternoon, there were big thunderstorms all round. One could see these forming. Tall, black-based white-topped cumulus clouds would drift slowly on the wind, sucking up energy from the warm seas, and pass by ahead, or astern towards the west. From others already formed, flashes of lightning lit the sky in the far distance, and thunder rumbled round the horizon of the shadowed sea. These brooding storms always made me nervous, in spite of the strange fact that very few ever came our way. They interfered with the winds, making them unpredictable.

That evening, we were caught up by a squall. Rain poured down as we ran madly before it, the sails creaking and groaning under the strain. The pressure on the sheets was so great that it never paid to try to alter the sail area piecemeal. It was best to lower the whole main to adjust it. Therefore, one tended to carry on. The inevitable happened. The wind rose above force five and the topmost batten splintered, leaving all the strain on the one already broken. Hastily, I dropped the main.

It was now getting too dark to see what I was doing, so I hoisted a shred of the main and used this to balance the mizen. We went on at hardly reduced speed. In some ways, the boat was running more easily. I discovered that the snag of my rig was that the big sail up forward tended to push the bows down, especially with the wind on the quarter. But my main task the next day was to get the mainsail mended, which took some time. It was not very satisfactory.

Two nights later, we were sailing along in a light breeze while I read a book below. Suddenly, there was a thump and the boat came into the wind. I came on deck feeling puzzled, to find that the main was lowered, neatly stowed in its lifts. The halyard, worn away by the continual motion up aloft, had snapped. It was against this that I had rigged my spare halyard. I was glad, in a way, that I had had a chance to use it. We did not have far to go.

On the morning of the day before we were due to sight Bermuda, I was woken up by a strange thumping noise. At dawn, I had retired to my bunk as usual to rest after the long watch of the night. I lay and wondered what it was. *Erik* was going well, and the noise did not sound like a ship. Reluctantly, I popped my head out of the hatch. It was my first whale. Ahead of us, it was lashing its enormous tail in the water, no doubt to remove parasites. I hastily went into the cockpit and altered course to clear it. It took no notice of us as we went past.

The next day, I looked out anxiously for Bermuda. It seemed a long time appearing, but I knew it was very low. Fortunately, we were approaching from the south side of Bermuda, which is clear of off-lying reefs. On the north side, there are great encircling reefs, and many a vessel, which has mistaken its position has run upon these reefs without sighting the land. It was a remarkable achievement, discovering the islands in the first place, since it is sometimes difficult enough even for those who know its exact position.

I sighted the land in the evening; it was some distance away. I could not understand why we had taken so long to close it. By my calculations, we should have been ashore by now. I put the cause down to some adverse current.

It was only later that I discovered the true reason. Due to a misunderstanding, and the fact that time means so little in the Caribbean, I had set out from Antigua thinking that the date was a week earlier than it really was. It so happened that it was mid-summer, and this did not make a great difference to ·the angle of the sun, but as the days went on, this difference increased. So by my error I had been some ten minutes out in my longitude, and, at the end of the voyage, I thought that I was nine miles further south than I really was. Out of such errors are shipwrecks made.

As usual, I had no chart for Bermuda. But I had looked at a chart before leaving Antigua. The approach to St. George's seemed fairly straightforward, but I decided not to try and enter that night, so we hove to under the lee of the island.

The next morning, there was a fresh westerly wind. My worst fears were confirmed when I came up within sight of the entrance to the harbour. It was extremely narrow, just a cut between steep rock walls. Undoubtedly, there was another entrance somewhere else, but, having no chart, there was no way of finding out safely where it was. In light weather, I would have risked tacking in, but in a strong contrary breeze, it was easy to lose control when tacking with the rig we had. I decided to go to Hamilton.

Fortunately, I had a road map of Bermuda, and this gave the lie of the land, while I looked out for reefs and dangers by eye and common sense.

Reefs, at first, can be scaring to sail among, and it is true that many vessels have been wrecked by running into them. Coral is hard and sharp, and can even slice the bottom off a steel ship. I was faced with tacking up a narrow cut without an engine, in a boat which could be difficult to tack with a crew, let alone single-handed. But now this idea had taken root, I was determined to do it. I had only planned to go to St. George's beause people said that Hamilton was too difficult to get to and took too long. Now I would see for myself.

The channel was well buoyed. It had been cut to cater for big ships. The reefs to starboard, however, were in places only just beneath the water. Because of the uneven set of my sails, the boat was often difficult to put about from the starboard tack. The boat would then fall off again in the same tack, heading for the reefs. Twice I had to wrench the tiller up and gybe the boat round in a circle, the keel seeming to skim the brown coral-heads suddenly appearing under the surface. Then we were through and into the lagoon. It was very choppy in there, the wind having got up fresh and making steep waves in the shallow waters. In the buoyed channel, there was plenty of water, but as we were tacking slowly up, often we had to go outside it. Then one had to watch out for those coral heads appearing as a brown stain in the water ahead.

That evening, I had to anchor off the beach. Sailing in coral-strewn waters at night is asking for trouble. The berth in the choppy water was very uncomfortable for a small boat.

Then the next day, a perfect wind to take us up the intricate channel into Hamilton. It was all well buoyed. Buoyage systems are fairly standard all over the world, which makes coming into strange harbours much easier. Soon, we were opposite the city of Hamilton itself. On all sides seemed to be little islands, with nowhere obvious to anchor.

I was hailed by a Boston whaler, speeding towards me. John Serle was its smooth-looking owner. He directed me to his own mooring, and looked after me very well. As he supervised a catering business for a boat-tour round the islands, he used to take me off to the island where the people disembarked for lunch and I would help them at their work. There were always a few spare hamburgers over.

We were only in Bermuda for a week. Despite John's attentions, I could not have afforded to stay longer. Even Americans find Bermuda expensive. That is expensive. With John's help, I stocked up with food and water, repaired the running rigging and did some work on the sails. I borrowed a moped, which is the standard means of personal transport in Bermuda, and toured the island. Bermuda is like a big park or playground.

Then it was time to go. This time, John had kindly given me a chart for going out, and he showed me a cut out of the harbour. He also advised me to try Ferry Reach if the wind was right.

The trip through Ferry Reach was well worth while. Bermuda appears to be an island, but really it is several, joined together by bridges and causeways. Ferry Reach was a passage between two islands like a narrow river. The wind was perfect. Soon I came to the first bridge where I hooted for it to open, and then onto the second. We came out into St. George's Harbour, and as night began to fall, we headed through the entrance and out to sea.

18. Towards the Azores

The night of the 5th July was spent becalmed off St. George's before a wind got up from the south-east, compelling us to head well to the north. On the radio, I changed to hear that there was Tropical Storm Arlene travelling up the coast of the United States. I wondered if the American accent meant that it was really Eileen. For some reason, not knowing annoyed me. The storm was not likely to harry us since it was reported six hundred miles to the north-west; later, a swell came from that direction.

We were now heading well north. The idea was that we were more likely to get westerly winds up there. In addition, I hoped to hitch a lift on the Gulf Stream about which I had heard so much. What I did not want to happen was to be stranded by calms in the Azores-Bermuda high pressure zone. I thought that if we kept well north, this was not likely to happen. As a precaution though, I had brought extra water in one gallon catering-size salad jars, the only containers handy.

The main difference from the trip across the other way was that I was now confident in my navigation, in spite of the fiasco on the last voyage — that was a mistake I would not make again. This had the advantage that the process of working out sights was a matter of course, but naturally, the thrill had worn off completely.

Navigation in the ocean is very over-rated as a skill, provided that the sun is reasonably visible. My particular method was rather old-fashioned. The most important and easiest sight was to take the altitude of the sun at noon. No exact time was needed for this, it only being necessary to wait for the sun to be at its highest point. Using corrections from the almanack and easy calculations, the latitude was found. This could be drawn straight onto the chart.

The most accurate way of finding the longitude was to take a sight of the sun when it was east or west, together with the exact time of the observation. Using a formula and the tables in *Reed's Almanack,* I would end with a figure which was my longitude and could be put straight onto the chart. It is known as the Longitude by Chronometer method. Not many people use it nowadays, although it is simple.

An even simpler method, although I found it only really accurate in tropical latitudes was what may be termed the Before and After Method. Its advantage is that it can be done at more or less the same time as the noon sight. A sight is taken, say, half-an-hour before noon is expected and the time noted to the second. The reading on the sextant is noted as well. Then after noon the same reading is set on the sextant, and as soon as this coincides with the position of the sun, the time is taken again. Exactly half-way between the two, with a simple correction according to season, is the exact time that the sun is at its highest. From this can be plotted the longitude. The tables, a chart, sextant and a radio for getting the correct time are all that are necessary.

I worked it out that if I used my Longitude by Chronometer Method for the moon as well, it ought to be possible to find the longitude with some degree of accuracy without knowing the time. But I never succeeded on the way across, and on the way back I was using an out-of-date Almanack — quite acceptable for sun sights, but not for the moon. Star sights with my plastic sextant I found quite impossible to take. I never needed them.

To cater for times when I could not take sights, I always noted down the course and speed at frequent intervals to give me some sort of guide. My log books were invariably ordinary exercise books, arising from the English Law of Not Seeming to Take Things Seriously, I suspect. In this, five narrow columns were ruled and the headings 'Time, Wind, Barometer, Course' and 'Speed' were put in. The rest of the page was a wider column called 'Remarks'. Anything note-worthy was put in here.

The Wind column gave the direction and estimated strength of the wind at the time noted. The direction was always the Compass direction — no allowance being made for the magnetic variation. It was easier that way, since the Course too was simply the compass heading of the boat.

The barometer reading was always put in, even though I regarded the information it gave as totally useless in the tropics. It made something to do. After all, taking an exact reading of something is a marvellous talisman against the uncertainties of the world, as scientists well know. My barometer was nothing elaborate. In fact, it was a wartime altimeter which I bought many years ago as a schoolboy from a surplus store. To replace the foot scale, I had pasted a card giving the equivalent pressure in millibars, which, of course, covered only a small part of the face. It looked most peculiar and makeshift, and just the sort of thing a schoolboy might make. It worked perfectly, and, whenever I could check it, was dead accurate.

The speed, of course, I had to guess. With a patent log which many yachts have, one would put down the distance run. I could not afford one of these instruments, and would not have bothered with it if I could. They are very good at tangling up with fishing lines.

I had, by this stage of the voyage, given up the idea of drinking salt-water. I never even used it for cooking. Instead, knowing that I was going to a part of the ocean where I might drift for days, I had gone to the trouble in Antigua of filling up all my old bottles with water, and putting them in the bilges. Each bottle held surprisingly little water, but there was a surprising number of bottles, a tribute to the cheapness of alcohol in Antigua, and the hard work we put into disposing of it. Many yachts have arrangements for catching rainwater, and with a sailing boat a system can easily be improvised by catching water running down the sails. As I never looked like running short, I never bothered. In parts of the world, too, where clothing is not needed, and where it rains fairly often, elaborate washing is unnecessary. One just stands in the rain.

For the first week, very little happened and progress was slow, though the wind had come round into the south-west. I got into the routine again of becoming a night-bird. This was easier with my marvellous radio which could pick up short-wave transmissions such as the B.B.C. World Service. This was broadcasting in the earlier part of the night. After my supper, I could lie in my bunk and listen to it. I never read books until the programmes were finished. This was to preserve my supply of books. Every quarter of an hour, I would look up out of the hatch to see if any shipping was about. I had discovered by experiment that, in reasonable visibility, even the fastest ship could not get too close in that time for me to take avoiding action. But it depended upon me spotting a ship's lights on the horizon without fail. Once or twice I failed to do so. For some reason, those were the ships that came closest in the end.

I usually had my light down in the cabin so that I could read by it and display it to a ship if necessary. Perhaps I should have carried one on deck too, but I seldom bothered to do so. Not having a light meant that I knew I had to look out without fail. To my mind there was something very unseamanlike in going to sleep at night, even with navigation lights blazing. Some ships with auto-pilots are said to do so.

If I was especially tired, or was getting sleepy towards the end of the night, I would set my alarm clock for a quarter of an hour ahead. For a single-handed sailor, I found that an alarm clock was an indispensable piece of safety equipment. The danger of shipping was the only one that worried me unduly throughout the voyage. You can survive a shipwreck with luck, but a direct hit by a ship gives you no time for anything.

This business of dodging ships was strangely unlike what I had imagined an ocean voyage to be like. Once I did a questionnaire which purported to tell me what job I was most suited for. The answer was that an outdoor life would not suit me, and especially to 'avoid something like the

Merchant Navy'. I seemed to be spending my time now avoiding the Merchant Navy.

By the 12th, the weather had changed abruptly. The wind was now westerly, the sky overcast, and it was pouring with rain. The wind increased strongly and soon I had only two panels of the mizen set, with only a tiny portion of the main to work the tiller. It was very rough. I had to put the washboard into the hatchway to stop the rain coming in. There was a narrow gap here to enable me to open the hatch and to give ventilation. The rain drove in torrents through the gap and poured down where the masts had loosened at the deck, filling the bilges with water. I had to bail this out, and in the process of pouring it away, the plastic bucket was whipped out of my hand and blown into the sea towards the bows. I decided not to commit suicide by trying to get it.

I had thought about the danger of going overboard in rough weather. At first, I had tied a line round the mizen mast when going forward, but this seemed to me foolish. I did not fancy being dragged behind the boat on a long line until I drowned. The idea I used later was best. A line was tied round the main mast up forward, and the end left ready in the cockpit so that I could tie it round myself there. That way I would always be dragged towards the side of the boat. A special harness would have been better, I suppose, but I never had to put it to the test.

During the next two days, the wind went round the clock, through north, then east, making us have to beat against the wind, then into the south-west. On the 15th, I captured some floating treasure. On the port bow, there was a bright orange object. I decided I ought to go and see what it was. There was a faint possibility that it could be some castaway in a life raft and so one is duty bound to go and have a look. I dreaded what I might find in such a circumstance, since I had already weighed up my chances of surviving in a life-raft in the middle of the ocean.

I soon saw that it was just a large orange polythene buoy. I did not pick it up at once, I am ashamed to say, having missed it at the first attempt, but eventually I got hold of it.

It seemed enormous. Still, I was determined to keep it. It might make a present for some service rendered by fishermen, and it was the sort of buoy which can also be used as a fender. The problem was one of where to put it. First, it was hung over the stern, since twined inextricably in the netting round it were strange rubbery sea slugs. I waited for these to drop off. Later, it was put on the foredeck by the main mast. It seemed enormous as I struggled with it along the side deck, nearly tripping over it and falling overboard. I tied it round the mast and onto the dinghy which lived on the cabin top. It did not improve the appearance of the boat.

I had now become resigned to the fact that the boat would always look a mess. This was not only due to my haphazard way of doing things, but also to the lack of space on board. Down below, things were not too bad, though everything looked extremely rough. There were now no covers on the mattresses, since these had rotted away ages ago and been thrown overboard. They were just bare foam mattresses three inches thick and cut to the shape of the bunks with a pair of scissors. Under the starboard bunk was a removable bit of bunk bottom like a lid. This covered the sanitary arrangements, simply a bucket. For obvious reasons, and for convenience, this bucket was kept in the cockpit. In the same place, on the other side, also easy to get at, was the paraffin and methylated spirits. These were needed for the primus stove and the Tilley lamp.

Cooking stoves I found a great difficulty, and certainly my struggles with them did not improve the look of the boat. The most successful one, because the most simple, was an old-fashioned Beatrice stove I found by chance in a sale. It had a large wick and burned paraffin. It was slow, but it could be lit without fail in a few seconds. For slow cooking of things such as stews and the inevitable curry, it was ideal. Unfortunately, it was not made of the right stuff to stand up to a life at sea. It met its death on the trip to Antigua. I put a kettle of water onto it, and it collapsed mortally wounded into a heap of rust. The remains had to be buried at sea.

The kettle also met its end soon after, perhaps out of

remorse. The handle, made of the same useless metal, iron, rusted to pieces. Thereafter, I used a pan for boiling water. This was rustproof, being made out of aluminium, and the space saved by not having a kettle was well worth while. After practice, it was possible to pour boiling water out of this pan into a cup while the yacht was heaving about, without pouring it over oneself. It was just a matter of timing.

The only stove left now was the Primus stove. This would nearly always play up, possibly because of the different grades of paraffin used abroad. I had still not succeeded in getting it to burn with a completely blue flame, despite frequent cleaning. The paraffin was carefully filtered before being poured into the stove. It was always an unpleasant task and was performed in the cockpit if the weather was suitable. A piece of the tissue was folded in four, then spread out to fit into the funnel. This was placed in the filler hole, which for some reason had been arranged so that to put a funnel into it, it was necessary to remove the rapidly rusting pan rest from the supports. It always spread a shower of rust over the boat.

The paraffin was then slopped out of the container bit by bit into the funnel. It took ages to soak through the filtering tissue, but eventually there was enough fuel in the stove. Fighting the motion of the boat, I would then juggle with the three things — trying to stop the stove from falling over before I could put the lid on, the container from falling over and pouring paraffin everywhere, and the funnel from falling down into the bilges as the boat heeled. The tissue was then thrown over the side to keep down the smell of paraffin.

The Tilley lamp was easier. I never had to bother to filter the fuel since it had a self-pricking device for removing dirt from the jet.

Eventually, the Primus pan-rest rusted to pieces entirely and had to be thrown overboard. Life was cleaner when it had gone. The pans had to be rested precariously upon the three supports. Sometimes, if I was careless, they would fall with a crash, tipping their contents everywhere.

My two-foot-long swinging galley shelf, made out of old bits of floorboard, was one of the most useful things on the boat. The stoves could simply be put on this with no chance of falling over, pans could be put onto it, and cups of tea or coffee placed on it without risk. Like everything else, it looked rough but it worked.

In a very small boat, and especially one so primitively laid out as mine, it was an enormous problem to know what to do with everything. Things were packed so tightly or in such inaccessible corners that I seemed to spend my time moving gear from one end of the boat to the other. Eventually, I became quite ruthless and I would pass an eye over every piece of gear to see if I could do without it. If I felt I could, any useful bits were taken off it, and it was then thrown overboard. It became a bit of a disease. When I had a spare moment, I would pass my eyes over each part of the boat and its poor little pieces of equipment in the spirit of Jack the Ripper. . . .

In the after end of the cockpit was a net containing all sorts of rubbish — old fishing lines and harpoon guns, bits of rotting cloth for mending sails, bits of line for lashings, spare sheets. Periodically, I cleared this out and threw half of it overboard.

The cockpit itself was taken up by the huge and heavy bulk of the inflatable dinghy. I doubt if I ever had the slightest intention of using this, but I was reluctant to jettison it. It had been a gift, it was quite valuable, and I had met too many people whose lives had been saved by these things to discount it entirely. Perhaps my feelings against it were wishful thinking.

Next to this dinghy was a collection of plastic buckets, which used to roll about when it was rough. The rest of the cockpit was fairly clear except for the inevitable tangle of lines arising from my primitive self-steering gear. The compass, of course, looked as if it had come from a museum and was the pride of the boat since it looked so primitive. I made a point of not cleaning its green brasswork.

On top of the cabin was my extraordinary dinghy. This

was simply tied on with lines passing through holes in the hand-rail-cum-hatch-sliders. It interfered considerably with the opening and closing of the hatch, and invariably shifted off its supports so that it was cock-eyed. To move the hatch, it was necessary to put one hand under the dinghy and lift it slightly. At first, this dinghy used to collect barnacles, unless I was careful to scrape them off before bringing it on board, and these smelt badly as they dried out. So I put anti-fouling on the bottom to combat this, and to fill up the leaks which developed in it due to teredo worm. This stuff smelt worse still. Its smell lives with me yet.

Down the side-decks were usually strapped spare bamboos or spare pieces of timber with which I was intending to mend the deck-edge. These deck-edges were so badly made that they were extremely vulnerable. On the rough trip to Antigua, one actually got washed off driving into the seas. I was not very proud of my workmanship. When I looked round the boat and took in its appearance, I began to feel that we were, as they say, riding on the rims.

19. The Azores

According to my chart, the Gulf Stream could be expected to be helping us on our way at a latitude of about 39° N the latitude of the Azores. It seemed very definite about this boundary, and I was not inclined to believe that it could be so sharp cut.

By the 17th, the weather was unsettled. The wind was from the south-west, varying from three to six, which is getting uncomfortable for a small boat. The sky was a uniform grey, and a thin wetting drizzle came streaming down the wind. Speed was only slow, about three knots, for in this wind, less sail could be carried and the big, roaring waves, even though on the stern, slowed the boat down as she rolled from side to side. It was nothing like the friendly trade winds.

The barometer too had begun to come alive. That afternoon it was at 1030 millibars. Two hours later it had dropped to 1020. In another hour it had risen to 1025. Two hours later it had fallen to 1017, and the wind increased again. Next morning, there was a tremendous deluge and the barometer began to rise again. I spent quite some time pumping the water out of the bilges.

With the rise in the barometer, came the north-westerly winds, still strong. It was becoming more difficult for me to keep to the north towards the Gulf Stream and it was impossible to check the position, with the sky so overcast. On the 19th July, the fourteenth day, I got a good position. My latitude was 38° 51° N, longitude 45° 43′ W. We must now be in the Gulf Stream. We had done a thousand miles, leaving eight hundred still to do to the Azores. At this point, the clock was put forward three hours to Azores time.

That night, there was a minor disaster. The stove had started to play up again and the jet was blocked. In trying to unblock it in the violent motion of the boat, the pricker pin snapped off, stuck immovably in the jet. I had no nipple key, which was foolish of me. I had got into the habit of not worrying about the Primus stove, always having my wick one in reserve. I looked through my resources. I had the solid fuel stove I had been given and a fair supply of solid fuel. But unless I could devise some other method, it might not last. We were approaching the part where I suspected there might be calms. Then our progress would really slow down.

Annoying too it was, that it should happen this very night. I was going to have the celebration meal of fried tinned chicken I had been saving up for when we were well and truly half-way. This had to be postponed to the next day, and I succeeded in cooking the meal over the solid fuel stove.

This day, there was really something to celebrate. I checked my calculations again and again, but they seemed to be correct. For I had my splendid radio which meant there was no trouble about getting time signals and the correct Greenwich time each night. In that twenty-one hour day, we had done one hundred and thirty miles. Our position coincided with a point on the chart marking the current as one and a half knots. But perhaps my navigation was out after all.

The winds now became more awkward, gradually creeping round until the following noon through north to east. They also dropped so that they were much lighter, averaging force two to three. In this light weather, I found that the alterations I had made to the sails, decreasing the area, had made quite a difference to *Erik*'s speed. In addition, the boat had not been anti-fouled and was gathering weed and barnacles at an enormous rate, thus slowing the boat down further still.

It was a continuous battle to keep north in the Gulf Stream, the winds, and maybe a current, continually pushing us south. Perhaps it was my imagination but I noticed a curious thing. There was a lot of shipping about now. We were obviously on a major route. When we were well to the north, presumably going with the Gulf Stream, nearly without exception all the ships were going our way. Further south, where a comparison of the day's run made me think that there must be eddies of current against us, most of the ships were coming west.

At the time, I regarded this as conclusive that the Gulf Stream was very clearly defined, merchant skippers knowing about these things if anyone does. A vast amount of money is expended on research into ocean currents, since, with the high cost of freight and shipping nowadays, a delay of a day can cost a company many hundreds of pounds. This was why I was always reluctant to hail ships and ask for help or directions, though many captains would stop their ships to ask if I was all right. Their jobs depend upon a fast passage, which was why I always appreciated such attentions.

By the 25th, the wind was east. *Erik* will hardly go to windward at sea, and certainly not in these light winds. Strange swells came from nowhere, lasted for a while as if there was a wind coming from some other direction, then would vanish away. These latitudes, too, were popular with porpoises. I used to yell and thump in the cockpit with my foot as they came past and they would turn aside to investigate this clumsy, noisy monster. After loafing around and diving under the boat, grunting as they came to the surface, they would swim on again.

This 'calm weather when I had nothing to lose by stopping for an hour or two, was ideal for sail-mending. The main especially was becoming more and more tattered. There was the part where the battens had broken. This had increased the strain on the cloth and was ripping up the sail by degrees. The problem was that the pull of the sheets on the topmost battens tended to bend them, putting all the strain on the edge of the sail. To combat this, I tied light line to the ends and this was extended to the peak of the sail.

The forward edge of the sail was in an even worse

condition. The front seam, with its large stitches and no roping, had not been strong enough. As a temporary repair, I tied cord from one batten to the other again, to take the strain of the cloth. This did not look any better, but it held the sail firm, and stopped the rips spreading through it.

The snag with the Chinese sail is that it is always fixed to the mast, and without dismantling everything it is impossible to repair the sails properly. Besides, there was so little deck space on the boat, that there was no room to spread the sails out to put patches on. The only way to get such a sail flat is to hoist it, and there are few more frustrating and perilous tasks than standing on the deck of a bouncing boat trying to sew a patch onto a sail. If I did such a trip again, I would have with me a little office stapling machine for fixing the cloth on. As a result of these difficulties, I usually tried to last out until making port, instead of making repairs to the sails.

The winds followed the same old pattern, moving right round the compass every few days. The wind would drive us down out of the Gulf Stream. Then fifty miles in a day would be good going and this was not always in the right direction. Later, when the wind allowed it, we would haul up again to a higher latitude. The day's run would increase to eighty miles or more.

Easterly winds were used to move north if possible, both because of current advantages, and because the further east one goes across the Atlantic the more likely the winds are to blow towards the south. If we were caught south of the Azores in such a situation, we might have difficulty in making up north again.

This continuous changing of our course, and altering the boat's helm to allow for the fickle winds started to take its toll. I found myself beginning to drop off to sleep at night. One night, I was wakened up by a tremendous thumping. I rushed on deck to see a ship passing only a few yards away. Indeed, there was a great deal of shipping about. I usually saw several ships every day, mostly at night time. Ships' lights in the distance are far easier to see than a portion of superstructure or masts passing along the horizon many miles distant. Often, I could hear the thumping of engines coming down wind with no ships in sight.

When progress is good, even when the weather is rough, the long hours at sea pass easily enough. It is when things slow down that the life becomes tedious. It becomes hard to know how to pass the time constructively. On a larger boat, I felt, with an easier motion, I would have been doing all sorts of repairs and improvements, but in *Erik* I could only do things like that when the weather was right.

On one such day, I decided to tackle that deck edge before the pieces of wood I had got for the purpose in Antigua were finally washed away. By this time, most of my tools were rusty, and the saw was virtually useless . . . so I threw it over the side. Then I attacked the pieces of wood with an axe to shape the part round the bow, drilled holes through with my rusty drill bits, put it into position, nailed screws in most of the way using a screwdriver for the rest, and planed off the top with the plane. The whole thing was given a thin coat of paint, using the remnants from my tin of red paint, which was then thrown overboard. Most of this had to be done hanging from a rope over the water to stop falling overboard. It must have been the most unprofessional carpentry job ever, and certainly one of the quickest. It did not go very far to fill in my time.

My bookshelf was becoming very empty after all those nights of reading. Books just could not stand up to the permanent dampness and by this time they had come to the disintegration stage. By the time I was half-way through a book it would be dropping pages and tiny bits of white stuff in a shower whenever I picked it up. I would then read it in a fever of impatience so that I could get rid of it in a watery grave. As the scattered leaves disappeared astern on the backs of the waves, I would look with sadness at the rapidly emptying shelves, wondering which to select for my next victim.

On the last day of July, it was calm again. I took the opportunity to change over the mizen halyard to the spare, since the old one had deteriorated in the sun. It had gone brittle so that twisting it made it dissolve into a shower of tiny pieces of plastic. This labour did not take very long.

We were now only two hundred miles from Fayal which was where I had been told to head for. The next day a good north-west breeze got up. We were now running down our latitude to Horta. It was a good feeling.

By this time, I was beginning to run rather low on methylated spirits. This is what I now used for cooking. The Primus being useless, I took off the burner, and made up a bracket out of stout wire to hold a little round tin. Into this methylated spirits were poured and set fire to, making a good flame. It was, in fact, more efficient than the original, for by pulling the bracket so that the mouth of the tin was closer to the pan and the flame starved of air, I could even do slow cooking.

Eating was not too important at sea, I found. I always took one or two foods which gave the necessary protein and vitamins. The rest was counted as a luxury. Besides, after living in the tropics, I had got used to living on very little. Breakfast, since the end of the porridge oats many months before, had been given up. I never missed it. Lunch was a snack, and supper was usually curry and rice, or stew. I took on board plenty of fruit when I could, and onions. Tomatoes were said to be a good source of Vitamin C, so I took some of these and rationed them out carefully. I never suffered from scurvy, nor did I expect to.

This food did tend to become rather monotonous, but, from experience I learnt that it was best to have it so, varied on the special occasion, such as Sunday, with something special. To have something special every night would not have helped. Hunger, I found, is the best sauce. It also keeps one fit.

In the small hours of August 3rd, a light approached on the port bow. I could not identify it, having none of the information needed, but I knew it must be Fayal. It was a beautiful run round the island, though under the cliffs on the approach to Horta it was tricky, the wind often dropping off.

Then we were left rolling helplessly with the sea belching and surging against the rocky foot of the cliffs not many yards away. Approaching along the harbour breakwater, strong gusts ripped down the mountains. But the island looked very pleasant, the houses more beautiful after Caribbean tin sheds, and the fields well-kept and cultivated.

At the entrance, a motor launch came alongside. A uniformed official jumped on board with his hobnailed boots without a word. There is nothing that makes the average boat-owner more angry than someone coming on board without permission. In this respect, I was average. There is good reason behind this seemingly foolish attitude. Occasionally, yachtsmen have had to fight for their lives against uninvited visitors who have come to seek whatever treasures they can find. This man climbed into the cockpit.

'I am the pilot,' he announced.

'I never have a pilot on board,' I told him. And yachts do not have to employ pilots when entering a port as most merchant vessels must.

'There is nothing to pay,' said the pilot. As this saying was music to the average yachtsman, and in this respect also I was average, I forgave him somewhat.

The wind was very fickle, and as the sails were extremely tattered, and the bottom of the boat was foul, our progress into the harbour was not spectacular. We had to tack, and while I tended the sheets and tiller single handed, the pilot leaned against the cockpit coaming and yawned ostentatiously. Eventually, he suggested that I got a tow from the launch which was still circling aimlessly around.

By now, I was determined that we should sail in if it took all day. Fortunately, it did not. A lucky slant of wind enabled us to sail in on one tack. I could then tell him to take the helm while I lowered the sails. We glided into our berth against the quay, the lines were thrown up to the inevitable bystanders above, and we were in.

There was then a long session filling in a green form, a session I made even longer by insisting on writing my name in full every time it was needed, and then the pilot was gone.

Here in Horta, I came across the Café Sport. A character
with a car drove me round there. The Café Sport is, in fact,
well known to all yachtsmen who have visited the Azores. It
is a sort of unofficial Yacht Club. The original owner is an
eccentric called Henriques. At the outbreak of the war, I was
told, a Dutch ship was in the harbour. It was impossible for it
to leave without being sunk, and the crew was stranded
without money. 'I get you everything you want,' said
Henriques. 'You pay me after the war is over.' For all those
years, he provided them with food and drink. After the war,
he was paid by the grateful company and awarded a plaque.
There are strong links with Holland in Horta. A Dutch salvage
tug is almost always on station there to go out to any ships in
trouble in mid-Atlantic.

It was sometimes embarrassing to go into the Café. Even
if I had already eaten, Henriques would often escort me into
a back room where a meal was laid out. It was quite
impossible to refuse him.

The smell over Horta was characteristic. There was a whale
factory in the next day. The Azores were one of the few
places where whaling is still done by hand, in rowing boats.
The nearest any of us got to seeing this was to go and watch a
whale being cut up. It was a revolting spectacle.

The hospitality of the Portuguese in Horta is marvellous.
Friends in another yacht had got to know a Portuguese
couple and I was invited along on outings round this
beautiful island. Peter, Henriques son, arranged for one of his
customers called Otto, to look after my needs. It was one of
his 'duties' as part of the club. All I needed now were
bamboos. Otto promised to get some, Peter promised to get
some, but they were a long time coming. Meanwhile, I sat
down on the quay and mended the sails, sewing patches over
the ripped parts, and deciding to keep to my system of lines
joining each batten together.

All this time, the boat was moored against the quay,
perfectly comfortable, thanks to the huge fender I had
picked up. The major discomfort was the crowd which
seemed to collect just above the boat, examining every move

I made. The only time they went away was when the girl on the boat up the quay came on deck to wash her hair. She had been to a drama school, so she did not mind. No one took any notice when I washed my hair. I took to a mooring as a refuge from the crowds.

All too soon it was time to go. I was running short of money, for I had cashed the last traveller's cheque of my never-to-be-used emergency fund. Although my parents cabled some money, I could not stay here indefinitely. As it was, I was decidedly sparing when stocking up the boat with provisions.

Also, I wanted to go back to England before the autumn gales began. The crew of the Dutch tug said I was already too late. This time of the year, there were north-west winds. One yacht, they said, leaving in the autumn, had taken seven weeks to do the twelve hundred miles to England.

As I still had no bamboos, a customer at the Café invited me to come to his greenhouse and help myself, which I did, although I could not see how I would now have time to put them onto the sails. Then two other lots came, one just as I was preparing to cast off our moorings.

Henriques, of course, had some food for me to take, the taxi driver who brought my bamboos gave me a great packet of tinned tuna fish, Otto gave me a bottle of wine. I could only give two conch shells in return to Peter and Otto. They were all I had to give. Then it was time to go. After a rainy spell, and northerly winds, the breeze was fair. Hoisting the sails, I dropped my moorings and we headed out of the harbour on the homeward voyage.

20. Home

Little did I know when I left Horta that 20th August, that the next voyage would be my longest. The wind was dead on the stern, taking us quickly through the islands on a north-easterly course. It is always gratifying to clear the land as soon as possible. Then there are no worries about running ashore.

Next day, there was a change of wind. It came round to the north-east and strengthened. Soon the sky was grey with scudding overcast, the rain streaming along in a wind which was pushing us well over, spray driving occasionally onto the deck. Knowing that it was useless to try and make progress against this sort of thing, I dropped the sails, but later hoisted just part of the main to steady us.

That night the wind still moaned through the rigging with that northern sound I had grown unaccustomed to in the tropics, and the rain poured down without stopping. I saw the lights of a ship, and it seemed best to put up the radar reflector I had been given so long ago. It was wired together and hoisted up the mizen mast with the spare halyard. Up there it clanked about happily, though later it stopped. The next morning, when I looked up at the mast head, the reflector had gone.

When the wind moderated, we were able to sail on a northerly course. The idea was to go well north to start with to a point where westerly winds were more likely to blow. We were going better now. In Horta I had swum down in the usual fashion to scrape off the barnacles from the bottom of the boat with a piece of wood. After the Caribbean, the

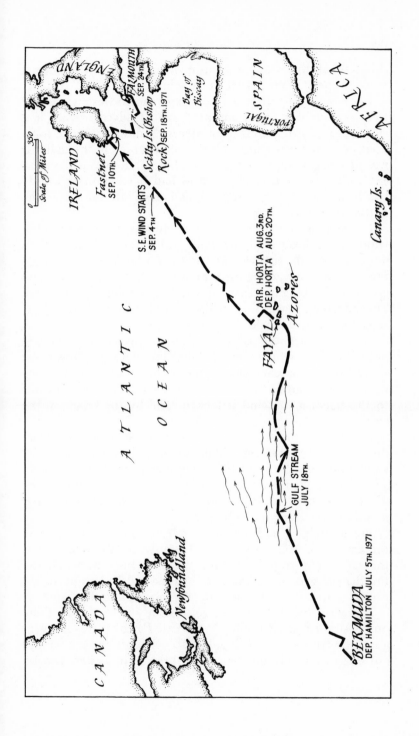

coldness of the water was surprising. But the difference it
made in speed made it well worth while.

Four days out, after a calm, came north-west winds. We
were on our way, then another spell of adverse winds and
calm, and at last a south-west breeze. It did not last for long.
That evening I was lying on the bunk listening to the radio. It
was just beginning to get dark. Suddenly, there was the most
extraordinary motion. *Erik*, who had been running calmly
before the wind, began to pitch and crash into the waves like
a fifty knot power boat.

I rushed up on deck to find the boat running before the
wind into a head sea. The wind had swung abruptly into a
northerly squall with violent wind and rain. With full sail up,
the boat was staggering into the waves. The sails creaked and
groaned, the bulging canvas threatening to split at the seams.
The unstayed masts were whipping and bending like fishing
rods hooked to a whale.

Hastily, I tied the safety line round myself and climbed
onto the deck which was bucking like a horse. Showers of
spray flew up on each side as the bows drove into the steep
waves. The main had to be lowered at once. But when I came
to the halyard, I found it locked solid by the strain on the
cleat.

I dashed to the stern to try to release the main sheet from
the tiller. Then the sail would swing right round with the
wind, and spill the wind from the mizen too. But these lines
also were locked solid onto the tiller by the pressure of the
wind. I looked up at the masts jerking in the wind. Any
moment something might break.

Fortunately, I had my quick release gear on the shelf in
the cabin – a knife. Using this I simply cut the main sheet,
the sail swung round, bringing the boat into the wind, and
the danger was over. Later, the furled sail had to be swung
round again onto its proper side, no easy task in that wind.

Not until the 30th did we get a steady westerly. By then,
our position was 480 miles N.N.W. of Fayal. It was not very
good for ten days of sailing, but to celebrate the fair wind, I
did one of my periodic clear-outs of the stern locker. The job

was complicated by the fact that my one remaining fishing line was tangled round everything. Sorting all this out, I hung the line over the stern to let it untwist itself in the water.

When I came to haul it in again a few minutes later, the weight surprised me until I realized there was a fish on the end. It was a tunny fish of perhaps ten pounds which had taken a liking to my piece of coloured towel, the bait. As it was evening and coming up to supper time, I felt compelled to eat it. Slaughtering it and cutting it up was a revolting job in my unaccustomed hands. I ate two fillets for supper that night, but there still seemed a lot of fish left. Eventually, I threw it away and never caught any more fish. The smell hung over the cockpit for days.

For four days, the south-westerly winds kept up. In that time, we made four hundred miles. It was excellent going. Then the wind changed. These were the last westerly winds for three weeks, though I did not know it at the time. My aim was to keep on well north if possible in preparation for the north-east winds I had heard so much of. But I did not expect to have much trouble with the last four hundred miles.

There was quite a lot of shipping about, and I always kept a good watch. The sense of this was obvious one night when I saw two red lights seemingly in the sky. They seemed rather faint and were moving from side to side. Then I realized that I was looking at a vessel of some sort. Two red lights, one above the other, is the signal for a vessel not under command — in other words, any other vessel must give way to her. The lights were at first on the port bow, then came on the beam. Dimly in the night I see the masts of a schooner as it rolled in the swell. There were no other lights on board, the crew obviously being asleep down below. No doubt it was a tunny fishing boat resting for the night. It is the sort of obstacle it does not pay to run into.

Early the next morning, the wind was east, just the wrong way. I did not want to go any further north since we were now on the latitude of the Lizard in Cornwall. I dropped sail to wait confidently for the wind to change to its prevailing direction of west, going below at dawn to sleep as usual.

Life at sea becomes very monotonous. Not much out of
the ordinary happens, since all the problems one has to face
are the same sort of problems all the time. This at least is the
reason I give to the fact that at sea I found I could do with
very little sleep. Four or five hours were usually enough each
day. Perhaps the cause was also my method of always
keeping watch at night. If one tries to sleep at night, waking
up every two or three hours to see that everything is
satisfactory, one does not sleep so soundly, however many
lights one can display on deck. Always the single-hander's
mind is on guard even when asleep, switched on like an
automatic pilot. During the day on the other hand one's sleep
can be far more profound and refreshing.

This particular morning, however, I was woken up by a
noise which stunned me for a moment, it was so unexpected.
Somewhere above my head a dog was barking. I thought I
was dreaming at first, since the noise was so out of place, but
then I went to the hatch to have a look. Fortunately, now
that I was in the comparatively cold northern part of the
world, I was dressed.

A few feet from my head, almost overhanging the boat was
the stern of a tunny fishing boat, obviously doing some tight
manoeuvring. On the deck was the barking dog, and if our
deck had been higher, I am sure that dog would have been
aboard by then. A fisherman, too, was obviously getting
ready to jump aboard. They were a little surprised to see me,
but explanations were out of the question since I could not
understand their brand of French. They were probably
Bretons. They simply waved and concentrated on extracting
their boat.

This had an extraordinary appearance. A long fishing rod
projected from each side for perhaps forty or fifty feet,
though there were naturally no lines trailing from these at the
moment. The boat was rolling heavily in the swell, the rods
alternately pointing towards the sky and dipping towards the
sea. For a time we seemed in danger of getting entangled, as
a great rod heaved about within inches of the mizen mast,

now one side, now the other. If it had caught under the rigging and nothing had given way, it could have plucked that mast out of the boat, like a pin from a pin-cushion. They managed to get clear, however, and went away. That evening, another fishing boat came circling round.

For five whole days that wind stayed in the south-east, light, sometimes very light. All I could do was to put the boat on the starboard tack and head up north, hoping the wind would change. It didn't. To make matters worse, the weather was miserable, a thin and almost permanent drizzle sneaking along on the wind.

On the night of the 10th September, I could see the beams of both Galley Head and Fastnet Rock lighthouses. We were off the Irish coast. Now I was back in European waters, at least I could identify lights from *Reed's Almanack*. These were two lights I never expected to see when we set out from the Azores.

The night was clear and the wind still south-east so I decided to see if I could make Cork. As usual, I had no chart, and from the list of buoys in the Almanack it seemed complicated, but I knew that in good conditions it should be easy enough to get in. We sped in fine style along the coast, but by morning, with not many miles to go, the weather became suddenly worse. The wind shifted more northerly so that we could no longer head on that tack along the coast, and the visibility became extremely bad, a misty drizzle cutting down the view to about a hundred yards. The land was nowhere to be seen, but we could not be very far off by now. Then the wind began to rise. Soon it was a good force six. It was obviously necessary to go about on the other tack. To lie helplessly in a strengthening wind near a lee shore I could not see, and having no idea of our true position, was clearly dangerous.

As we clawed our way southwards again, I eased off the wind so that it was partly on the beam, risking some of our distance offshore for some added speed in getting away from that coast. There was a nasty moment when the murk cleared for a few seconds and there was a great black headland in our

lee with white surf beating against it. I could imagine with
the blow of every wave upon *Erik*'s hull that we were bearing
down sideways onto the danger. But our speed carried us
clear of the land and I did not see that rocky bluff again. It
was plain, though, that Cork was now out of my plans.

That afternoon, when I thought we were clear of danger, a
curious smell penetrated the cabin. It was like the smell of
chlorine. There was also that subdued rumble which comes
from a large turbine ship. Rushing on deck, I was in time to
see the stern of a huge liner vanishing to the west, its
superstructure just visible. Ahead of us was the great
light-green turbulence of her wake. As we crossed it, I tried
to calculate how many seconds we had missed the liner by.
Even if I had been on deck, I doubt that I would have seen it
in time to take avoiding action.

I had now decided that it would be wrong to put into
Cork. We had set out to go to Falmouth, and to Falmouth we
would go. I began to review the situation.

One of the reasons for heading for Cork was that we were
running short of essential supplies. There was not much food
left, only a few pounds of rice and some dehydrated foods
and soups I did not set much store by. There were some
assorted tins. More important than food, I had now nearly
run out of paraffin for the lamp. I had not taken much of
this on board to start with, since the lamp was the only thing
that used it. I had to re-organize my whole lighting and
cooking arrangements.

After the incident with the Primus on the way to the
Azores, I had taken a dislike to the whole idea of pressurized
paraffin equipment. Memories of hours of struggle with the
things suddenly rose up in a revolutionary hatred.

'Abolish paraffin!' I cried.

In the Azores, I had bought bundles of candles and these
were used in one of those large salad-cream catering jars
brought from Bermuda. It made an ideal candle lamp. A wire
handle was fixed round the rim, and the lid was punched
with holes. Like this, with two candles inside and hung from
the lower-most mizen batten, it made a good windproof

riding lamp, though the candles tended to drip in the motion of the boat and burn too quickly. With the lid off, it burnt well in the cabin too, and I was very pleased with this simple and foolproof lamp.

The only snag was that I had bought far too many candles in the Azores. These must, I think, have been made of whale tallow since they burned with a clear white flame but a revolting smell. In order not to have too many left over at the end of the voyage, I got into the habit of using them in ridiculously extravagant quantities, keeping two candles going all night. Again, because of the motion of the boat, these burned wastefully, depositing great quantities of wax on the bottom of the jar.

The stove too would soon be out of action, not that I had much food left, but I would appreciate a cup of coffee now and then, I thought. Until I realized that I was running out of this too. . . . The stove was run on the methylated spirits' principle invented on the way to the Azores. It was simple and foolproof. It was also extravagant on alcohol. Although I had got in a good quantity, there was not much left.

Then I put the problem in perspective. The trip to Falmouth could not possibly take more than a week, and even this was a ridiculous length of time. Two days with a good wind and I would be there. Besides, if I was actually in danger of starving I could always hail a ship for some food, though I was determined not to do such a thing. Although the wind was still fresh and the drizzle and mist unceasing, we were going on a tack well east of south. We were heading towards the Scillies and when the wind changed, we should not take long to arrive.

The wind did change. It changed to the south-east and stayed there, though often it dropped off light to almost nothing. Now that we were to go south-east, it could not be worse. We fought down to the latitude of Bishop's Rock in the Scillies and slowly struggled eastwards. Always that wind was in the east.

By this time too, after the windy weather we had had, the main was in a state not far short of unspeakable. The top

three panels were almost in ribbons in places. Setting the sail
was like trying to stop light with a net curtain. Eventually, I
had to abandon these three panels. It was done by lashing the
third batten down to the yard where the halyard was fixed. I
thought at first that this would rip the sail where the wire
fastenings hold the battens to the cloth, but to my surprise, it
did not happen. But we now only had half the main in light
winds in a boat whose bottom was quickly fouling up. It was
not a cheerful situation.

Incredibly, it took six days to make against those light and
contrary winds to the Scillies. All the weather forecasts I
would listen to avidly, in the hope that they would forecast
westerly winds. They did, but the winds never came. When
the forecasts were right, they only succeeded in telling me
what weather we were having at the moment, always seeming
many hours out of date. It was infuriating.

Painfully, we crept through the Scilly Islands to within
sight of Bishop's Rock light. Then the wind dropped off
again. Soon the coast was miles to the north as we tacked in
the easterly wind. All we needed was a south-easterly for the
next tack and we would be home.

Unbelievably, the wind changed to the north-east, and
dropped almost completely. We had had south-easterly winds
without a break for a fortnight.

How slowly the time passed now! I racked my brains to
think of things to do, to plan, to think about. I planned my
next boat – poor *Erik*! – if a time would come when I
should have one. How it would be larger, with a rig that
would steer itself by a simple lashing of the helm. How it
would be small enough for a man to handle and have that
feeling of independence of others on the shore, yet large
enough for two at least. Or how about a square-rigged ship,
and take a fare-paying crew to sail around the world?

Such future plans seemed too fanciful. So as I lay, I
designed inventions. An anchor that would never foul, an
anchor which warns you when it drags, an automatic
gearbox, a fuel-less engine. . . .

Ideas came easily. Perhaps they are coming too easily, I

thought as I lay there. Perhaps they are like dreams which seem sensible enough when dreamed, but when the dawn comes become ridiculous. There was no-one to tell me.

It was also time to think of what I had been doing. For this was the last act in our voyage. In a way it was refreshing, and I realized now the urge which prompted me to sail back and not to sail to other goals. It put the voyage behind me, for it made a circular tour and not an endless voyage in which I might drift on for ever.

And was it worth it? I wondered if I had changed, and, if so, how. For now the challenge of the voyage was gone, I was left only with the fruits of achievement to use or throw away as I wished.

What of that love of the sea which many claim to have, was it there? I never had it, but nor did I ever hate the sea. One thing that strikes you more and more as you crawl over its huge and wrinkled face, is how alien and how impersonal the sea is, a world where you do not belong. You are on the sea, and the sea is under you, and under the sea is a life you can hardly guess at in its watery otherness. This is why you feel that the sea can hardly touch you. . . .

Angrily, I would tear myself away from all these foolish thoughts. It would be easy to become fanciful when given such hours to brood. Fortunately, I had hunger to come to my rescue and give that bitter touch which keeps things real. For now my stocks were very low, and we still had not arrived. . . .

There was almost no food on board. I would make a sort of soup once a day and that was my lot. There was hardly any fuel either. The alcohol and paraffin had gone long ago, and so had my candles. I had taken to using the solid fuel stove but the fuel for that could not last for ever. The candles too were finished.

My only asset was the melted candle grease. I broke this out of the jar and split it into pieces. Then I twisted some wire round a piece of wick made from stranded rope so that it would sit in one of my little round tins. The wax was then melted into this bit by bit. I now had a candle and a stove.

This method had to last until I got in. Although I had run out
of coffee, there were still some tea bags, and those were very
heartening to a stomach which had not eaten any proper
food for days.

The lamp I had made was not good enough for warning off
shipping. I had to keep watch all night in what are some of
the busiest waters of the world. My nights on watch would
have been relieved a little if I had felt that I could listen to
the radio, but its batteries had to be conserved. I began to get
extremely tired.

Tiredness at sea is very dangerous. It is partly made up of
lack of sleep, and partly from exposure. The sufferer
becomes punch-drunk and it is difficult to take the right
action at the right time. By the 21st of September, after
nearly thirty-one days at sea, we swept past the Lizard
lighthouse in great style and headed up the coast towards
Falmouth. We were nearly home. Then the strong spring tides
running just then began to ebb and we were swept back
towards the Lizard. I decided to tack out, and tack in again a
bit more to the east. The alternative to this mistaken action
was obvious to me as soon as it was too late and we were at
the end of my outer tack. I should have dropped an anchor
to stop drifting with the tide, then when the tide turned,
raised the anchor and drifted calmly on the tide into
Falmouth. It was obvious. As a payment for this mistake, I
spent three more days at sea.

With the calms out there off the Lizard, came fog. It
meant that I had to watch during the days as well as the
nights. The fog was continuous, giving no chance for sleep.
Often ships came close and I had to be ready to hoot back at
any hooting ships. Ships which hoot are those without radar.

I had two things to help me at this time. The first was my
little bottle of amphetamine tablets which I had got more
than a year before from my doctor for just this purpose. With
their aid I had next to no sleep for three days.

The second was my hooter itself, which always cheered me
up. It was made from a conch shell I had picked up on a
beach in Dominica in the Caribbean. To turn it into a horn I

had chipped and filed away the end to make a trumpet-like mouthpiece. It made a marvellous noise.

Whenever I heard a ship close by, I would dash to the cockpit, raise the conch to my lips, and blow — only to give out a feeble bleat. This was always liable to make me collapse with laughter. I never really mastered the art of getting a good hoot the first time.

On the night of the 23rd at midnight, the wind changed to the south-west. It started light as if it hardly meant it. Then it strengthened. In a few hours, I was anchored inside Falmouth Harbour waiting for the dawn to give me enough light to see where to take the boat.

Just as I was getting ready to move, a fishing boat came up. There were reporters on board. It seemed that the papers had heard about my voyage, and the long delay of my arrival had whetted their appetite even more. My own appetite was whetted by the fact that I had only two soup cubes left. There was nothing else.

I had been expecting to go ashore quietly and head for the nearest fish and chip shop with what money I had left, then have a long, long sleep. But although I did better than fish and chips, there was a long day ahead. It led eventually to *Erik the Red* being at the Boat Show, and going to the Exeter Maritime Museum. Such brief fame was looked for by neither of us, and I could never take it seriously. It was hardly the point.

ROBIN HALL'S LETTER
ON THE DESIGN OF THE KEEL

CHEAM,
Surrey.
Sept. 16th 1965

Dear Donald,

I hope I haven't kept you waiting too long. In theory, the casting of your keel is simple, but in practice you are bound to encounter snags of one sort or another.

For the following reasons I do *not* advise casting the keel directly into the deadwood.

    a)   The connection between concrete and wood is most important for a good job, and I am doubtful as to whether your suggestion would be satisfactory. You will appreciate that the lateral force on the keel is large — hence the connection must be as efficient as possible.

    b)   Any balls up you might make casting in-situ will land you in trouble after the concrete has set.

Hence I think it would be better to pre-cast the keel, and connect to the hull with bolts. The best way to do this is to use bolts passing from top to bottom through the keel as follows:—

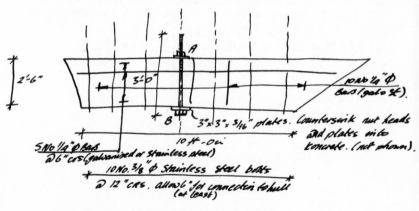

The advantage of this type of construction is that the bolts have a three-fold use.

    1)   Connection to hull.

    2)   They will act as vertical reinforcing bars.

    3)   Tightening down of nut A will impart a prestressing compres-

sion into the concrete, making it stronger in bending and less likely to crack.

The bolts may be expensive (10/-d—£1), but must be stainless steel for corrosive resistance. The distribution steel ¼" ϕ Bars 26" crs. should be either stainless steel or galvanised. It is highly likely that minute cracks will appear in the concrete (not necessarily visible to the naked eye).

Sea water will therefore reach the steel, and if ordinary mild steel were used, whether in bolt form or normal reinforcement, expansion of bars by rusting would shatter the concrete within a few months.

Mix Proportions and Casting Procedure

1). *Cement.*

Use sulphate resisting Portland Cement, to guard against sulphate attack from particularly magnesium sulphate.

2). *Sand.*

A well graded sand (beach sand *not* adviseable).

3). *Coarse Aggregate.*

Could use a $\frac{3}{8}$" max. coarse aggregate to give normal concrete, but in this case granolithic concrete would be better for the following reasons.

1) 'Grano' has a harder surface (not necessary stronger in bending) and does not present such an attractive surface for barnacles as ordinary concrete. The latter is more difficult to clean.

2) 'Grano' can be polished with a power sander to give an excellent anti-drag surface.

Advise ¼" granite chippings.

4). *Proportions of 1, 2 and 3.*

1 part cement: 1½ Sand: 3 granite chippings (by weight).

5). *Water/cement ratio.*

The consistency of the concrete must be such that it is *just* workable, i.e. not too wet. If it is too wet, you will get leeching out of the sand, and *also* a loss in strength. If too dry, you will experience difficulty in placing, resulting in 'honeycombing'.

Thus use a water cement ratio of 0.50 i.e. 1 gallon water to 20 lbs ct. If this makes mixing difficult, add a *little* more water, but don't drown it!

6). *Formwork.*

Best to use plywood (hard-board will bow too easily—. Make as rigid as possible, and grease the inside to prevent sticking.

7). *Placing of Reinforcement.*

Form a mesh so, and drop into formwork. Make sure there is at least 1½" cover to the steel at the bottom and at all sides (not possible at extreme after end).

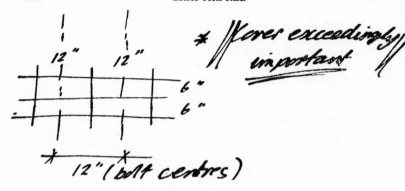

The bolt holes will come alternately with the verticle ¼" Bars. Box these out with $\frac{3}{8}$" φ polythene tubing (grease thoroughly beforehand), and leave a 3'-0" length to pull on after setting. Also box out with wooden blocks the rebates to bottom nuts and plates.

The ¼" rods can be bound together with steel tying wire, and must be kept in position in the formwork with mortar or concrete spacer blocks (don't use bricks).

8). *Placing of Concrete.*

Tamp the concrete with a stout metal bar to ensure a dense surround to the reinforcement. All air must be expelled; proper compaction is essential not only for strength but also for correct external appearance.

9). *Curing.*

As the concrete sets, so heat is omitted. Counteract the effect of this by swathing exposed surfaces with wet hessian. This is particularly important after striking the forms (leave in forms for 24 hrs.). Ideally do not put keel in seawater before 28 days, by which time the concrete will have developed most of its strength. It will, however, only be necessary to cure with damp hessian up to 3 days.

Remove polythene tubes after 1 day (may take more than one person!).

10). *Grouting of bolt holes.*

When you have placed the bolts in position, pour cement grout (water and cement into the $\frac{1}{8}$" anular gap) to bond into the concrete.

⸌ Flush off the bottom edge of the keel by fitting up the bolt hole rebates with cement mortar, 1 part ct. to 3 of sand).

I hope these notes are of some use to you. They may not be comprehensible, so don't hesitate to question.

I think there has been some discussion on this topic in either Yachting World (or Monthly). It might be worth a try.

Yours,
Robin